FROM THE MOUNTAINS OF GOD

By

T. Maxwell Smith

CONTENTS

v

INTRODUCTION

I dedicate this book to those who suffer from drug addiction, alcoholism, and immoral sexual sins. This is to establish a written memorial to my spiritual journey. It is a written record of my experiences with Yahweh, the God of Israel. My life testimonies are here to share, encourage and instruct others to repent of their short comings, sins, and inequities.

I encourage you to follow Yahweh. Being a Christian is sometimes not enough to fill that emptiness or void that will cause us to use those crutches in life. Don't be caught in the river of life drifting to the ocean of HELL. Remember God did not leave. On the contrary it is us that are separated from Him by Sin.

Do not rely on your own strength and wisdom when dealing with SIN. Be assured that without Yahshua, Jesus Christ, the Messiah, and the Holy Ghost there is no discipleship or fullness in Yahweh, my God. If you won't settle with salvation only, this book is for you. Salvation is instant but to be a true follower of Christ will take the rest of your life.

A-Man

Chapter 1

෫ඞ ඞ෭

HAD I KNOWN GOD BEFORE?

As a young boy, I knew God was God as He touched my life and thoughts. It was from these mountains deep in McDowell county of West Virginia that I first realized He would communicate. His love and grace has been more than sufficient to forgive me, as I became a man. Had I known God before?

I would lie on a spur ridge (the finger of a ridge) overlooking the Tug River or Dry Fork river and knew He was God. He began to talk to me, (my heart) and assured me even as a child He was real. Later in life he spoke to me verbally on a mission trip in Brazil. We will get to that later. He is present, He is God.

I began my search for God at this time or was God reaching out for me? If He truly was real, He would reveal Himself to me. Abba is not just a name as I came to know but He is really the Alpha and Omega. He is God. He is the Great I AM. He is our Father in Heaven and the Kingdom of Heaven is at hand. He through the spiritual man in me began to appear, as I would open up my heart to receive His presence. It is this hole or void in my heart I first realized His Holy presence as He entered my tiny soul.

In the summer breeze high on a mountain, I would lay in the carpet of green moss an occasionally pick and munch on a red mountain berry. Mountain teaberries as we knew them as kids of the Appalachians were a little red berry that found its way amongst the rhododendron and mountain laurel. There are plenty of plant life, insects, deer, and squirrel and of course snakes. This includes the aggressive copperhead and the seen too late rattlesnake that would leave his memory of the encounter. I'll never forget that peculiar rattle or buzzing sound, Man there were some big ones in the hollers and around the rock piles our dads had massed up when clearing the bottom lands near the creeks.

I'll never forget the manly sport the grownups enjoyed. They would have us kids uncover the rock piles while they shot the snakes as they would come out or flee. Many times I wasn't sure they hit the snake or my bare foot toes when the dirt would fly up. I guess that is why I wore shoes as long as they would last or until they became too short for my foot as we only got shoes mostly on Christmas and they had to last all year. New brogans were a welcome to most of us mountain boys. Times were hard then also.

My favorite mountain stream was Harmon's branch which offered great swimming holes to a kid in the hills. I sure wish we had that fancy underwear the city folks had. They would ware these when they came down to join us in a cool dip in the branch. We spent our summers damming up the flow of water and then of course as soon as it rained we had to do it again. Mountain boys did not bother with those city customs. Yes, I know it is called skinny dipping.

Most of our dads were coal miners and to be poor meant nothing to us. We all seemed poor and this was an accepted way of life. I spent many days there on that mountain ridge and often pondered about God. Being poor and before television was common is a blessing to a kid in search of his destiny or his origin.

In fact, I was probably fifteen years old before I saw my first TV back in 1955. The only ones invented and available were black and white. Of course to be politically correct there might have been color TV, who knows? It was on a Saturday night that my cousin Butch and I were invited down to watch it, (TV). There weren't many sets in Iaeger, our little mountain town at that time. We were excited and heard there might be some girls there also added to the adventure. To receive a signal, there had to be a transmission line stretched to the top of the mountain, probably three thousand feet straight up to the mountain top. Of course the lines had to be cleared regularly or you would lose signal. The signal generated in Bluefield W. Va. Was fifty miles away. And of course American Bandstand was on. Man what a show. We could watch how to dance and watch those city folks do their thing, like rock and roll or something like that. Had a preacher tell me dancing was wrong and I think he is right, especially the belly button kind? Later we could get a signal from Huntington a mere 112 miles down highway 52. On good day you really could not see much on the screen except an outline of someone and lots of snow as we called it. I did not think highly of this "TV thing" and besides I could not sit down the first experience I had to watch.

You must understand this was on Saturday night and we had heated water for the number two wash tub and I was testing the water before getting in and as I bent over, Butch was ironing his jeans and he branded me with the hot iron on my necked butt, Wow!, did that hurt. Butch was my hero and of course he was a little older and a star running back on the football team. To make things worse after I finished jumping around we decided to put lard on it, which sealed in the heat.

He explained, Mommy always did that for his burns. All I know is my bottom paid a price but later in life, I would get even.

I would often talk to God in a childlike way not knowing what to say to someone I couldn't see but I knew He was there and would listen to my thoughts not always words at this time. Sometimes only God knew or understood what I had to say. I wondered why I seemed to be the only one with this secret friend that was faithful to meet with me on that ridge top. I even used a language that no one else could understand. I felt like I had invented a new language. English was not one of my favorite things. As this designed language that God and I knew but no one else understood became one of my main sources of communications in prayer. Of course, I now know that it is called an utterance before God. I often wondered what He (God) looked like and why He would have any interest in me. I knew He was really my closet friend. I felt secure in this newfound friendship and love. Of course I now know we were created in His image.

Even as I write this, I shed tears of shame that my life has not been worthy to receive this miraculous gift. Why can we not keep our childlike faith? Is it because Satan and sin entered our life? Each one of us must deal with this question. It is by God's grace and the death of our Messiah on the cross that secured my salvation and given me a second chance. When He arose after three days it proves that my Friend defeated death two thousand years ago. He knew me even before I was conceived. It is awesome to seek His face and walk in amazement that He could die for my sins as the perfect sacrifice of His sinless nature. Had I known God before?

When they hung my Friend, Jesus on that cross I am reminded He was on a hill. Each time I see a hill or mountain I think of the cross my friend spent His last moments asking Abba, Father God to forgive them for they know not what they do. My faith began on that Mountain of God. Later in life I would meet Jesus again and you know what, He didn't change but the sin in my life was a barrier to His presence. Once again I opened up my heart and He was faithful to come back into my life, this time as my Savior. His grace is sufficient once you accept Him as your Savior and Friend. My friend, believe upon the name of Jesus and receive your free salvation. Live for Him, He died for you. It will take the rest of your life to earn the title of disciple or follower of Christ.

Now that I am a man, I look back on my life and it seems so long ago I meet my friend on that ridge in West Virginia, which is truly the Mountains of God. However, it is only a whisper in eternity. I know that I am still that young boy and have regained my childlike faith. He listens to my prayers and I know His voice now. It is not what people may think but what you know to be true. God is real. We were made or created at birth with a hole or void in our heart so that God can enter in and communicate. It is this void in our heart that is the doorway to our soul. Our very intellect, emotion, and love for Jesus must be received through this door way. His Holy Spirit will direct His will in our life. We truly can walk with Him in the garden or He will be with us on the mountain top if we will but only believe. We are fortunate to live in a country that God has blessed. We can worship and live the good life, thanks to the many men and women who have paid the ultimate sacrifice for this privilege. God is the Great" I AM" and best of all He is an Omni God. He is with each of us and lives in us through the Holy Spirit. He has truly blessed America.

HE IS THE ALPHA AND OMEGA
HE IS THE BEGINNING AND THE END
HE IS THE BREAD OF LIFE
HE IS THE CHIEF CORNERSTONE
HE IS THE CHIEF SHEPHERD
HE IS THE CHRIST
HE IS THE GOOD SHEPHERD
HE IS THE HIGH PRIEST
HE IS THE HOLY ONE OF GOD
HE IS IMMANUEL, GOD WITH US
HE IS JESUS, YAHWEH SAVES
HE IS YAHSHUA, THE MESSIAH

HE IS THE POWER OF THE LIVING GOD
HE IS KING OF KINGS AND LORD OF LORDS
HE IS THE MEDIATOR BEFORE GOD
HE IS PROPHET
HE IS RABBI
HE IS SAVIOR
HE IS THE SON OF MAN
HE IS THE SON OF GOD
HE IS THE WORD
HE IS GOD IN THE FLESH

Abba Father your Word is anointed and now Oh Lord I ask you to anoint my words, my thoughts and all hearts to be open to your Holy Spirit as the unction makes itself known.

Make solitude loud in the eyes of those searching for peace, joy, and love. Bring forth that small voice that assures the listener you have heard their cry from the wilderness of life. Without God you are truly in the wilderness.

GODS INVISIBLE DEITY CAN BE SEEN IN SOLITUDE

In the shadow of the cross lies our direction in this life. With the shadow of the cross an image will be seen. This image is of course cast by the absence of light in that area. The Light of the Father will cast the shadow of the cross upon His followers. We must remain in His Light and let the shadow be seen by all. Always cast your shadow while facing Yahweh our God to be seen as your sermon to others. It is the best message you can portray.

Receive His Holy Spirit and Cast your shadow to the entire world. Allow His invisible deity to be viewed by others in your shadow or walk. The best sermon ever preached is to the shadow of your life and how you live your life.

Search for the solitude of prayer and experience the deity of God. Baize in His Glory Cloud illuminated by the Light of the Holy Ghost and be made complete. God the Father, God the Son, God the Holy Ghost in trinity will complete your humanistic walk and give you the promise of eternity. Salvation to eternity is instant once you accept Jesus, the Messiah.

When Jesus was removed from the cross at sundown, Gods inspired Word became our Light in the shadows.

As a young boy of twelve I worried when I heard another miner was killed in the mines or the saw mill had someone hurt again. My Dad worked night shift most of the time at Bear Town number six, a coal mine not far from our house. Being the eldest child my job was to take care of my younger sister and brother, which I failed at miserably most of the time. By this time Mom lived in Tennessee. Even though no one seemed to be there for me or us, God always protected us; was someone praying for us? I know the answer now is "Yes". Many in my family offered up prayers and served as intercessors for three young children and a Dad who worked hard in the coal mines. This unfortunately is the growing up life in the coal fields of the Appalachians in those days. It is still this way today except most of the jobs have dried up but God is still there for those children that play on the ridges. I urge people of the mountains not to give up but to trust in God. He is still there for you. If you are from the Mountains of God or the farms, or the flat lands or the cities, God is there for you. We are all God's children.

My foundation and beliefs can be traced back to that solitude on a mountain. It is here I first knew God and began the search for His fellowship. I can say I always knew God existed but where was He? There was no constant church fellowship in my life. I knew there was a Bible, which was proclaimed Gods Holy Word. I was told my grandfather on Moms side of the family was a preacher and was pounded, (received goods instead of money). By the way his name is Reverend Tom Robinette who is with my Friend, Yahshua now as are most of my people in West Virginia buried in the Roderfield cemetery or at Baileysville.

Life style, heart attack, or black lung killed my Dad when he was fifty nine. The doctors said it was a heart attack. Most of my uncles died an early age on this side of my family but they seem to live forever in Mom's clan. Eighties and nineties are common. In fact at this writing Mom is a young ninety and will be ninety-one in March of 2012.

My grandmother Smith would send me to church with a sock full of dimes, which represented her tithes. She did not see well and always seemed old. This was the local Methodist church in Iaeger. It was always so quite during the service and all I can remember was the silent sobs, which I did not understand. They tried to get me to sing in the choir and I remembered just moving my lips the times I tried. I would still have a heart attack to think of being in a choir. However I could now speak or preach to hundreds with the message of the gospel of Jesus Christ. I really could not get into that choir and had no idea why I was doing it. Granny use to tell me I would be a star in her crown and I had no idea what she meant. She blessed me and told me I would see the world, which was my boy hood dream. I can tell you my passport book has been filled and pages added since God is back in my life. I have been out of the country over a dozen times in the last five years. I heard a preacher say not to be a pew warmer and brother; I can say that description does not fit me. I have been to several counties and states doing the work of the Lord in the last five years. Physical effort is satisfying but God will use those vessels that will step out and spread the Word or be a witness to the great commission. If you exercise in the spiritual gifts you will be used by God that I can promise.

I use to get nervous in front of a group when it was time for that book report in school. Now I get excited to speak to hundreds or more because it gives me a chance to tell them about my Friend I meet on the ridge overlooking what God had put before me. You see Jesus is personal to me. He not only died for all of us but He is there for us when we are down in the valley as well as on the mountaintop. His presence manifested through the Holy Ghost is as real as blackberry cobbler and ice cream. He lives today to those that believe.

What is so good about this Friend, Jesus, there is a whole lot of words written about Him in the New Testament of the Bible. His Word is final and His truth is real we know He fulfilled the Old Testament making it complete and is the Messiah, the Son of God. Renew your mind daily with that childlike faith and be restored by His forgiving grace. What He has done for me and many like me He will do for those with an open heart. Take time to find a solitude place, be still, and listen to God. (Be still and know that I am God) If you search for Him, He will find you. We are created in His image and are His children. Our battle here on earth is not against flesh and blood but against principalities, against powers, against the rulers of the darkness of this world, against spiritual wickedness in high places. I like to think of myself as a spiritual being on a short humanistic journey and Heaven is just around the corner. Someday I can worship my Friend and fellowship in the Garden with God. I will proclaim Holy, Holy, Holy. May I remind you that when you have a conversation with God that is in the natural, not supernatural. Prayer is the key to enter His Kingdom.

It is mentioned in Ephesians 6: 12, (NKJV) be warned that Lucifer (Satan) himself is a fallen angel. He knows all the tricks and weakness of humans and is a worthy foe. In the book of Ephesians 6: 11-18 of the (NLT) guides us and directs us to resist the devil by claiming these verses. As we read the following words allow them to become your prayer and incorporate them into your life. Use word substitution when you study the Word of God and place your name or those you pray for in presence tense as you call out to God.

We are told to put on all of God's armor so that you will be able to stand firm against all strategies and tricks of the devil. For we are not fighting against people made of flesh and blood, but against all the evil rulers and authorities of the UNSEEN world, against those mighty powers of darkness who rule this world, and against wicked spirits in the heavenly realms. Use every piece of God's armor to resist the enemy in the time of evil, so that after the battle you will still be standing firm. Stand your ground, putting on the sturdy belt of truth and the body armor of God's righteousness. For shoes, put on the peace that comes from the Good News, so that you will be fully prepared. In every battle you will need faith as your shield to stop the fiery arrows aimed at you by Satan. Put on salvation as your helmet, and take the sword of the Spirit, which is the Word of God. Pray at all times and on every occasion in the power of the Holy Spirit. Stay alert and be persistent in your prayers as all Christians everywhere should do. I urge you to be specific as you pray and this will make a huge difference for God to open these doors. God will shut some doors and open others. The Word should be spoken in order for the Holy Ghost to act upon it. Our God is a Spirit and must be worshiped in the Spirit. One of my favorite verses is found in John 4: 24, (NKJV) God is spirit and those who worship Him must worship in spirit and truth. In Matthew 6: 24 (NKJV) we are told no one can serve two masters; for either he will hate the one and love the other, or else he will be loyal to the one and despise the other. You cannot serve God and mammon.

With the miracle of birth we were born into sin as outlined in the book of Genesis. God's plan was interrupted by disobedience and became sin. As you can see we were created by God, a deity unseen and invisible to the human eye but real just the same. You can also see that Satan, a fallen angel took up the corridors of the darkness and operates in the unseen realm also. We serve either the light or the darkness. Jesus is the only way to return to the truth and the Light of God.

God has given us the power to resist the devil and do good. When we accept Christ and learn to worship God, you will know the devil is under your feet and not stalking you from behind. As we praise Him for our situations and not in spite of bad times we invoke spiritual warfare. Victory is in Christ. God has never lost a battle. I beg of you to trust my Friend, Jesus. Our spiritual growth is a progressive venture in life and even though we may be emotional at salvation, we must learn to crawl before we can walk. As babes in Christ we start out on milk of the spirit until we can digest the meat of the Word.

MAKE ME FISHERMAN OF MEN

Growing up on the river bank of the ole Tug River afforded a kid the opportunity to be a kid and know what it meant to be a child of God. I would run my trot lines before going to school each morning. For you that don't know what a trot line is, it is a heavy line or cord stretched from one side of the river to the other and weighted down by rocks usually, tied at strategic points to keep it submerged against the flow of the current. I would re-bait the hooks and take the fish off and of course tie them up, (you fisherman know this term) and then sell them in the community later.

We lived across from the mining community of Red Bird. This was of course higher up the mountain than my river bank home and of course on the other side of the river. Here was a setting which later led me to Christ. As I fished the river and tended my fishing lines I learned to be a good fisherman; it was necessary to be consistent and obedient. This meant I would have to wade the current with no flash light and only the light of dawn. These habits became my training for life. The fear factor is removed as you learn to trust in the Lord. What person would even consider doing this type of adventure? Most likely a kid with nothing on his mind except catching fish, becomes obsessed with doing whatever it took to be a fisherman. My reward was catching fish. Now I am a fisherman of men.

I learned by trial and error to stretch my lines to use the favor of the current to place them in a suitable location. This is much like being in the favor of God and using the Holy Spirit as our current of life. He will show you where to be in life. His guidance is un-questionable if you learn to hear His voice. I urge you to trust in the Lord for not only guidance, and courage but for the correct direction to proceed in life. We must stretch up our hands in surrender and ask to be in His favor. The lines must be weighted down with rocks to prevent the current from tangling you lines on the river bank much the same way we must be rooted in the Word of God to keep our life from becoming tangled in Satan's domain. Since the days of my childhood I have fished in the Amazon of Brazil for the peacock bass as well as the piranha. All of the fish down there have teeth and of course quite different than the ole Tug River. This is only an example where God will take you. Trust in His direction and the desires of your heart will be realized.

I was in a church service on May 3, 1959 at the New Hopewell Baptist Church, in Knoxville, Tn. when I heard the preacher Jerry Tillman say, "if you will come forth and open up your heart He will make you a fisherman among men". What happened next is only a blur as I literally ran from the back of the church to the alter. I could not even say my name for the outburst of tears. As I accepted Christ as my savior I had no idea what was happening. I did not grow up in a church but I knew it was my Friend I had meet so many years before on that mountain of God. I had never given my life to repentance or asked God to forgive me of my many sins. That day seems like yesterday in my memory and I still weep with joy to be counted a part of the Kingdom. Hallelujah! to the Lord of my life. Oh God, I missed you so, and I know it was I that went away for you are faithful to be there for me and now you live within me.

There was no doubt in my mind when I gave my life back to God I already knew Him from the mountains of West Virginia. God did not go away but it was I that had drifted from His presence. Even a child can be consumed by His Holy presence and know that He is God. Jesus said, "We must be as a child to enter into the Kingdom of Heaven ". That mustard seed of faith is all that is needed to believe as we progress from one level to the next as we serve Yahweh the God the Bible.

The fact He would make me a fisher among men only confirmed that I should move on to God's work. No one could have been more excited to know my Friend, Jesus was calling me into His ministry, Wow!-make me fishers among men. What an exciting task before me.

The Lord knew I loved to fish but now it was for the souls of men in place of fish.

You know, as I remember Jerry the preacher, I pause long enough to remember my drill instructor on Paris Island. Sgt. Hamilton is another name that was burn into my memory. These two names have never been forgotten. The name of my Friend drafts these names as He is my Savior and I serve Him forever.

At this writing I'm not a pulpit type preacher but just give me the opportunity to witness for the Lord. Yes, I am in the ministry to do His will in my life. My true passion is missionary work and minister to the incarcerated prisoners in the state prison of Morgan County Correctional Facility here in Tennessee. This is the ole Brushy Mountain Prison for those of you familiar. The great commission to spread the gospel of Jesus Christ gets me excited even at the ripe ole age of 71.

As I reminisce and review my walk with the Lord I truly can't remember when the seed was planted or was I born with a measure of faith? Why some more than others? I probably do have Jewish roots long since hidden by time. But I can tell you the world of my God is real and He has confirmed and amplified my faith. Can you believe this started with a boy on a mountain top and his curiosity to know where he came from and why His Friend was there for him? I have since learned He is there for anyone who will be sensitive to His presence. After you are able to pray the sinner's prayer, the Holy Ghost will become your guiding light. This will be the source of your power as you become rooted in the Holy Bible which is God's Holy Word.

This identity crisis is real to many people. It is common to mankind. How can a child talk to God and get this answer? It is the same for anyone. Search for God and He will find you. We have a perfect example in my Friend, Jesus. He is the Son of Man and also the Son of God. He is born of a virgin and was sent to die for our sins. This is for all mankind to the Jew first and to the gentile. He is the perfect example to pattern our life. Once you accept Jesus you have and will become the people of God. I know longer suffer an identity crisis. I know who I am and my purpose on this earth. If you feel incomplete and no direction or purpose in life I suggest you fill the void with Christ. Make Him your friend or make Him your husband and establish an intimate and everlasting connection. I am not just a Christian but a follower of Yahshua, the Christ.

God's people will inherit eternal life and we do serve a living God. We are heir to the blessings of God. He is the Son of God (Jesus) and defeated death and arose on the third day. As Peter proclaimed in the book of Acts during the day of Pentecost what the Prophet Joel speaks. There will be an outpouring of the

Holy Spirit. We shall see signs and wonders. He tells us that the sun shall be turned into darkness, and the moon into blood, before the great and the terrible day of the Lord comes. You still have time to repent (change your mind) and seek the Lord for salvation. His grace is abundant. He saved me and He can save you. Don't refuse God and spend eternity in Hell.

I am reminded of another incident while my family was visiting relatives in Huntington, West Virginia (the first time I remember seeing a four lane highway). I must have been a teenager because I was awed at the cartoons in color seen on the TV. This is not what I remember from my past experience with watching the tube. I had an opportunity to fish the Ohio River even if it smelled of petroleum. I had to walk to the shore line across the dikes. The fish weren't cooperating so I began to talk to God, my Friend. I know now this was wrong to test God but I had a green hornet rod and reel bought on time at the Legato store back in Iaeger. That's right Mr. Legato would let you buy on time since he knew my Dad and we lived a rock throw from the store. I wanted to try it out on a big fish. I said to God, "If you are real let me catch a fish". I said a little prayer trying to help Him out and baited my hook with enough bait to choke a horse. I was fishing for catfish or really anything that would bite. I cast my bait as far out as possible expecting to catch a big fish from this huge river; the biggest one I had ever seen. I cast up river so the current would let it settle to the bottom without getting hung-up. I waited and waited but had no hint or indication of a nibble. It was getting late and I knew there was a God but where was the fish? Time was up so I began to reel the line in so very slow giving the fish plenty of time to see the bait. It seemed like an eternity bring in the line. I wanted to catch a fish and I had put God to the test. I prayed the whole time for God to allow me to catch a fish and confirm His presence. What happened next is nothing short of a miracle.

As I lifted my bait out of the water which was gone, I saw to my surprise a small catfish smaller than the hook I used to catch it. It was not snagged but its tiny mouth was where the bait had been. It had actually bit the baited hook. Praise God, my Friend was with me and heard my prayer and demonstrated He is real to those who believe. I haven't tested Him again and I know now even that time was wrong. I was on the milk of the spirit so Lord forgive me for my un-belief as I reeled the line in. God revealed His power to me as He allowed me to catch a fish. Remember to be specific when you pray. I did ask for a fish and not a large one. As I turned the little fella loose I thanked God for His faithfulness. This was truly the fish that God sent.

BUTTING HEADS WITH THE BULLS

Yes, His protection will follow us and go before us. The Angels of protection are there even when our good judgment or choices become lost in our sometimes not so smart decisions. When I was still on the milk as a babe (new Christian) and am reminded of an incident in my early walk with the Lord. I decided to test my new found faith. I have always been afraid of bulls and especially the large black ones that seem to know when we are in their territory.

It was a warm summer afternoon and I was driving my old car in the country. As I looked to my right out in the field I saw a herd of black bulls. I prayed Lord give me courage to approach the bulls and protect me. I stopped the car and crawled through a barb wire fence. They took notice of me as I walked toward them. Some had horns and all seemed like elephants in size. The only prayer I could muster was Jesus be with me.

As the distance became less and less I began to really pray. Was I really going through with this and was it worth it? I fell to my knees as they approached. Not one but the whole herd came forth. It was too far and it was too late to make a run for it, so I knelt to the ground as they finished their approach. So here I am in the middle of the field surrounded by a herd of black bulls, big ones. On my knees and low and behold here they came so I got down on all fours and they came over to me and accommodated my jester by putting their head against mine and pushed me backwards through the grass all over that field.

Glory be to God, they did not hurt me but seemed to know I meant no harm and they just wanted to play, which they surely did. I was definitely out weighed in the match up, so I just arose and walked back to the fence as they followed. God was there for me. My fear was removed and my faith was increased. Lord forgive me for doubting your almighty presence. I know now the Bible says not to test the Lord but to have faith. He has always been there for me. God is good, all the time.

If you are going to the Olympics with your walk with Christ you need not only to believe but begin your training with the first step. If you are a young Christian, race to the Word of God and graduate from milk of the spirit then be filled with the Holy Ghost power of God. He will make you fisherman among men and allow His vessel to sail many rivers, seas, and oceans. His destination for you will to be a fisherman of souls lost in sin that they might be returned to the Kingdom and not be cast down that river of fire headed straight to Hell. Hell is not a curse word but a real place.

As we go through life it is important to fast and pray; to pay your tithes; to spread the gospel of Christ and to be a witness for Him.

We must live every day expecting His return which is growing near. May I remind every born again Christian to not only fellowship with Him but take time out of your schedule and draw upon childlike faith and know He is the Great I Am. Call time out and separate yourself from this world and come into His presence. Seek purity and Holiness in your life. Turn the TV and radio off. Turn the cellphone off and turn your heart on toward the Holiness of God. Believe with all your heart, strength and mind and God will levitate you and fill you with His Holy Spirit.

Your Mountain of God is as close as your prayers. It doesn't have to be eloquent words or man's proper language in can be the language you use when you run out of words and have only those thoughts of your heart. I will assure you God will know whatever language you must use. This connection is from the heart which is your spiritual source. This is the doorway to the soul. Yes, our flesh, soul, and sprit is intertwined and this is what makes up us as a human creature—Gods creation. He gave us the choice to choose right from wrong.

As a child I didn't understand the church or its function. I had friends that attended church but it stopped right there. I was too busy growing up. Most of my time was spent fishing, hunting, playing on the river bank, climbing trees to see how high I could get before the limbs would break and going to the mountain. We even skipped school on opening day of squirrel season or did they close school, I don't really remember? My excitement as a child came from just being a boy, and my time of solitude on that spur ridge overlooking the rivers. I use to think how big God must be to control all of the things I could see. The world for me was so beautiful and God had given it to me. I use to pretend He had given me all I could see. What in the world could you do with a river or mountain except to see what a boy would see? God had put this before me to show His awesome power and glory. But what could a boy do with these thoughts. My imagination was wild but would people believe God talked to me? Yes, and He will communicate with all of us. As I told you I do know God's voice as He directs my path here on earth.

LIFE IN THE "HOLLER"

One night I was awakened by a knock at the door. Dad was gone to work at Bear town #6 at the coal mines near Bradshaw. My younger brother and sister had moved to Tennessee with my Mom by this time so I was alone. At the door stood my best buddy, closer to a brother of course and he was bleeding from buck shot wounds. Yes, we are related.

I knew he was up to no good but why I had not been with him was a mystery. When you saw one of us the other was not far away. To this day we don't talk about what happen. He had swum ole Tug River to get to my house I guess but it was no time to ask questions. I needed to stop the bleeding first. I certainly could not take him to the only doctor in town. He knew my Dad and lived across the road from my grandmother.

Not related to this incident I once wrecked my little 50 model ford drag racing and tore down 75 feet of Dr. Clark's picket fence down. Paul, another wild friend was with me and as I saw him sliding out the passenger side of my hot little ford in that first roll over, I just could not hold on to his winter coat sleeve. Needless to say he spent that Christmas in the ole Welch Hospital recuperating. Had he not had on that coat he might have really been hurt. Paul is gone on to be with the Lord now and I had to replace the fence one board at a time.

Meanwhile back at the ranch as we some-times said, (from watching cowboy movies) on with my story:

I forgot to mention the other friend but he was bad to the bone and had not been out of the Marine Corps long and of course he made his escape. I wonder if it was his Marine Corps training or fear of the new Doctor Smith in town.

Meanwhile back at the kitchen operating room once I got the patient calmed down and the bleeding stopped we decided going to the doctor was not an option so I called on my boy scout training (joke of course) and opened the refrigerator door for the moon shine anti-septic. I think I persuaded him to take a swig first as an anesthesia.

I gathered up my surgical instruments. One single edge razor blade and one nut picker, the instrument of choice you use to pick out the meat from the nut shell. I applied a little 180 proof shine to the wound and made a small incision. Then I took the nut picker and plucked out all of the 12 gauge shot I could reach, at least those near the surface.

He is still kicking to this day and I visit with him often. He is still not happy with the sur-gery as there are still a few shot in his head. So I missed a few but the patient lived, ha!

Forgive me guys but I'll never tell your real names of course you know who you are. Times back then make a different kind of man.

Muscle cars, moon shine-the real stuff made up the holler, hunting, fishing, and a general sense of adventure were the back bone of most of us hill billies. Actually we were not hill billies but were a continuation of mountaineers carrying on the tradition of our fathers. There is a definite difference. Hill billies are from the flat lands and we are born with one leg shorter than the other which permits us to travel around the mountain without a limp. Life is still pretty much the same in the Mountains of God, where the real mountaineers live.

We married the girl that became pregnant and got a job. Work was not something to get out of or an option. Yes, we had commodity cheese and butter furnished by the government you could get when your family was down on its luck.

The miners would go on strike as unionism for safety reasons and to bargain for higher wages. Not all the workers were in the union but would honor the strike. This was when unions had real purpose. You didn't hear about OSHA, might not been in place. We needed unions then and they helped form America.

This was the America I grew up in. Honor was a hand shake and an attorney wasn't needed very often. You bought a house to own and it became a home. We didn't borrow money unless we paid it back. We learned to appreciate things but things did not own us. Those that had land raised a garden and canned food for the winter. There were no super stores and we had a company store (Island Creek Coal Co. I think?) Located at Bradshaw owned by the mines that would extend credit in fact you didn't even need money since they would accept script (company produced trading money). The script was only good at the company store. This is probably not legal now.

Christmas was a new pair of brogan shoes. It was not uncommon to see someone going barefooted when the first snow came. Some people still lived in log houses with dirt floors and walked to school. I use to stay with Joe and we even dug coal out of the hill side for the fire place. We used a horse to pull the sled back to the log cabin. Buttermilk was the drink of choice so I just did without. Education was more than book learning it was learning about life. Fear was not a by-word. There were no gangs or drugs, just moon shine and that turned out to be a mistake.

School was neat back then. The boys could fish during recess and I think Mrs. Higginbotham, (sixth grade) looked forward to this time of rejuvenation. We did give her a hard time but she was well liked. Not like the substitute teacher who just walked out after Donald threaten to throw her out the window. I preferred fishing in dry fork since the rivers meet behind the school and hospital waste was dumped in the Tug. I even snagged a set of tonsils on my trot line once.

A lot of my class mates went on to be teachers. I wonder if they remember the good ole days. Playing hooky was just part of going to school for most of us. We didn't have to go very far to skip class. Actually just behind the school was a great place to hide and do whatever. Kids now days just think they have fun. Of course it might not have been this way in the flat lands. We were mountain boys and a different breed of cat. Smoking ducks (used cigarettes butts discarded) was the big thing if you wanted to be cool. Twenty cents was hard to come by to buy a pack of lucky strikes or camels.

Of course Red Man chewing tobacco was necessary when you played football. You had to spit fast and dodge quickly in order to blind the guy in front of you. It seems like I got sick every game as I just could not chew without being sick or was that I swallowed most of my cud.

Ask anyone from West Virginia, Kentucky, Virginia, Tennessee, North Carolina and the list goes on, we are the true mountain hill billy type of this country and God made us special and equipped us to be who we are- mountain people.

I'll never forget the feed store owned by the Bottomlys. It set next to the railroad tracks. We would gather and open the back doors to play blue grass music until some would even have heart attacks. It is a wonder no one got hit by a train which didn't even slow down. Of course I speak from experience if you were sitting on the tracks you could feel the vibration and fall forward before the train got to the store. Not saying we were drunk but you did not see many whisky finders in those days. We just slept where we fell without going to jail in fact we were encouraged to sleep it off. You could elect to walk home since most lived around the curve and curves went both ways.

As I remember my boyhood days on Gods Mountain I could always feel His presence. The simple touch of a spring breeze and the many smells associated with the mountain where I meet my Friend saturates my memory bank of His wonderful love and grace. I was alone as a boy but never lonely because He is always there for me and still is to this day. His very connection with me is as close as prayer. God will fellowship with you as you grow in His wisdom. He is the same today as yesterday and tomorrow.

When I journeyed from the high place of God, He was on the river bank with us. We didn't care much for shoes in warm weather and I can still remember the warm mud squishing between my toes as I explored for snakes and turtles. Sometimes we would get bitten by water snakes. They didn't usually bring the blood. Some I'm sure were not to be played with. To be bitten or not to be put excitement in my life. You had to learn how to handle them of course. Probably wouldn't do it now.

I know Mom would not even touch my clothes to wash until she supervised the ritual of me emptying my pockets. Yes, I always had fishing worms, frogs or snakes in my pockets. She used the washing machine that had the two rollers used to ring out the water and then of course she would hang them on the clothes line. You couldn't wear them until you shook the little black cinders out that came from a passing coal fired steam locomotive pulling a load of coal. I often wondered where all that coal went.

Once in my grammar school days I filled a cigar box with my collections of (snakes) and took them to school. Of course when I forgot them which I had placed under my desk, the kind that had a place for your books, they got out and the next morning they didn't ask who brought them to school. They always paddled us guys but not the girls. It was like they didn't have a butt or never got in trouble.

I have four grown kids now and others that just call me Dad, or Papaw. May I remind men that we do not have children and that if a child honors you by calling you Dad then let them become your children. I am sorry for my life style and at times a dead-beat Dad. It is my wish and prayer that my children forgive me as I have forgiven my parents. My sermon now is how I live my life. My walk with the Lord is one of dedication and sincerity. The generational curse is broken. Once again I give thanks to my Friend and Lord, Jesus Christ that I am now a born again alcoholic. He delivered me instantly and now I serve Him daily. The addiction is gone and His grace gave me another chance. The load is light for He will carry you and the weight of the load.

THINGS ARE CHANGING IN THE HILLS BUT GOD HASN'T

On a recent trip back to the mountains of West Virginia for a school reunion, I had the opportunity to watch the last football game to be played at the ole Iaeger High School my alma mater. This was to commemorate all those in attendance, past and present. This includes my parents with Dad being in 1935 and Mom in 1938. I finished in 1958 and to add insult to injury I spent more time getting out of Mrs. Boland's (my Aunt) English class than I attended. I learned to type only because that is where a lot of pretty girls or should I use the phrase "hotties", were present. I think Aunt Blanch started the school since she even taught my Dad and Mom, Wow! And Mom is 90 at this writing. My sister Brenda even attended school here. Oh, by the way my Dads name is Merton, which he picked out. That is another story. The school is to be torn down after years of flooding which has caused mold and mildew in the building. A new school has been constructed in Bradshaw which will accommodate Iaeger, Bradshaw and Big Creek areas.

I can say this, when coal was king we had more Cadillac owners per capita than anywhere in the US. Moonshine was the drug of choice and honor meant something. We served in the military, some by draft, but most as volunteers. College was far removed (no Pell grant) unless you were willing to study to show yourself approved. God was a solemn choice we made. This was an undisputed right move. God and country made us grow to become Mountaineers always. We had our problems but life in the mountains taught us a toughness not found when we came to the flat lands as fate directed. A hand shake did not require a contract, an attorney or a witness. We are a people proud to be called a Mountaineer and money (ain't) everything. Honor, respect, truthfulness, and character still mean something to this day. As the ole guard is replaced by the new we find unification somehow in all the stages it presents. The mountains we grew up in are producing more off-spring but somehow things are not the same since God was removed from our schools and government. We see drugs, crime, obesity, immorality and chaos in our country. Our lawyer-politicians are among the most corrupt in this hemisphere.

Why have the new generation not realized that God is the only answer to problems in their personal lives? We as parents can claim responsibility. We might not have grown up with prayer in our homes but we are not as far removed as this generation. Those of us that have searched for God until He found us should become intercessory for those that haven't been found. Each home should contain its own church and secret place where they can have communion with God. Bible reading as a family is a must to enforce our beliefs in God and to tell the true story of Jesus, the Messiah. To walk in the Spirit is an oneness with God and simply means He is forever present in our mind and soul. This can only be done by believing upon Jesus and that He arose on the third day from the tomb. Flesh and its products, lust, pride, anger, jealously, etc. will be replaced by righteousness. This purity of heart and our body will become the dwelling place of our Lord, for He will return. Keep His temple Holy, for we can't serve two masters. Study the Holy Word to become an informed citizen of this world. Nothing has changed since mankind was created by the spoken Word of God. It should be every Christian's desire and goal to learn as much as we can about the personality and character of God. The book of Genesis depicts man's creation and his fall. It is here we find that the devil or God requiring a human soul to operate within. One is for good and the other is for evil. The choice is ours. The choice brought on by sin when Adam and Eve partook of the fruit of the tree of knowledge of good and evil. Sin has always been the very thing that will separate us from God.

When sin is not corrected, we will suffer eternal death in Hell. We are given that choice to repent (change our mind) and live our lives for Christ. This daily task is a choice of good and evil, right or wrong choices. This is to do or not to do the will of the Father. Since we are both human and spirit this constant battle and turmoil is within our soul.

It is so simple to do well, or choose right over wrong and live under the guidance of the example set by Jesus, the Son of Man, and the Son of God. We must walk in the Spirit. Our daily breath must be in connection with God, to do His will. Begin our days and end our nights in prayer and supplication. Study the Holy Word, the Bible of our God. It is here we will find the truth, direction and fellowship required to remain focused on the Light Christ brought into the darkness that surrounds us. Help those that God is calling home. Be a witness unto the world of the good news of Jesus Christ.

Your sins are forgiven. Jesus paid the Sin Debt for all of mankind for eternity. He died a horrible death as He was crucified on the Cross, which marks the beginning of Christianity. God sent His only begotten Son to die for you and me. His sacrifice as the Son of Man, Son of God more than proves Gods love for each of us. Jesus lived in the flesh and was tempted as all of mankind and set the example for us to live by. He lived a sinless life and died to pay the sacrifice and on the third day arose from the tomb to show He is truly the Messiah.

Do you want to live for eternity? Never to experience death and fulfill what Gods plan for you on earth is. It is possible to receive power (Holy Ghost Power). First you must ask God for wisdom, understanding, and knowledge to equip you to be in oneness with the Spirit. We are both human and spirit and once you receive Christ in your life and decide to live for Him, simply ask God and you will receive this Holy Spirit presence. I encourage you to read the Book of Acts.

The power of the Spirit in Jesus' life authorized Him to preach the Kingdom of God and to demonstrate Kingdom Power by healing the sick, casting out demons, and setting the captives free. The same Spirit Power in Acts 2 gave the same authority to the disciples. The Book of Acts is the story of the disciple receiving what Jesus received in order to do what Jesus did. Hallelujah! to the Lord. Seek and you will find for God has already called you. Develop this uniqueness of your calling. God will not only reveal your call but will show you the way. He does not always call the qualified but He will always qualify those He calls. I am an example of what God will do for His children.

CHAPTER 2

❧ ❧

GOD WILL SPEAK TO THOSE WHO LISTEN; BE OBEDIENT UNTO THE LORD

I was on one of my early mission trips to the Amazon region of Brazil down in South America and it was there in Manaus God spoke these words to me verbally. He said, "My son it is time", and the voice came again and He said for the second time, "My son it is time". The sound came from the left and up at about a forty five degree angle. It was the voice I had not heard since I was on the mountain as a young boy except in 1959 when he forgave my many sins and restored my salvation. I had no trouble knowing the meaning what God had spoken; "To be involved fulltime in His life, even doing missions".

I was having difficulty getting time off from work to go on mission trips. So on my first day back on the job I told my boss I was going to quit (obedience) immediately. As

I explained the reason he understood and being a Christian man counseled me. They let me take early retirement. After my Friend spoke to me I knew it was time. In fact I was at a crowed table having our (R&R) before the flight out the next morning. No one paid any attention to the small voice I had just heard. I have not looked back or regretted making the decision to follow Gods direction.

The guys at work seemed to understand as they were mostly Christians. On the official day leaving this good paying job at the bomb factory on May 5, 2005 I received a part-time job the same day that allowed me to pretty much work at my own schedule. This part time position paid most of the missions cost. This is of God.

That very same day I was slain in the Holy Spirit and received the power of the Holy Ghost and this didn't happen in church. There was no music as a matter of fact I was in the Shoney's restaurant parking lot in Oak Ridge, Tn. With my friend Jonathan and we were praying for some people after eating. The awesome power of God came down. I have never experienced anything like that. We were in my Saturn SC1, a three door compact auto, with straight shift and the emergency brake between the seats. I tell you all this in order to paint the scene that happened.

I knew Jonathan was praying and he began to talk the Holy Ghost prayer language, at this time my Godly language had been only to myself but the unction moved on me and I began to visualize the person I was praying for and began to vocalize with my spirit and all at once the power of God came and IT through me between the seats and into the rear seat. The force held me down for what seemed like quite a time. I remember hollering for help as this was something I had never experienced. I wondered why my buddy would not come to my rescue and then it was over. I managed to work my way back to the front seat wondering all the time how I got in the back of the car. It took several minutes of maneuvering to get back under the drivers wheel. I was literally on my back between the bucket seats and into the rear seat. I weigh two hundred pounds. This was an unlikely feat for me in the natural to get by the console, emergency brake and straight shift mechanism into the back seat.

I asked Jonathan what had happened to me and he had no comment but knew I had just received the "Baptism of The Holy Ghost". Yes, I received the Holy Ghost Power on this day and to those who have yet to progress into this realm I urge you to believe and have the faith for it will happen. We are called to obedience.

God is calling His people to carry their share of the Cross. It is not the weight but the burden of souls at stake. How much does a soul weigh? Only God knows but I can repeat what John the Baptist cried in the wilderness, the Kingdom of Heaven is at hand. He proclaimed repent and be baptized. We must align ourselves to accept Christ and live to follow His footprints to the trails end. It doesn't matter which mountain or valley you are in or on. God is there for you.

This time my journey with the Lord is complete partly because of my obedience but mostly because of His Grace and Mercy. I lived many years in a back-sliding condition.

Now I sometimes arise at 3:00 am to jot down my thoughts as the Lord places them in my heart. This will seem unusual to a lot of folks but my burden for those lost souls is sometimes over whelming. I owe my very existence and life to God, my Friend as I am a born again alcoholic.

Some of this I am about to write is insane, especially here in America, in this great country and it is the greatest country in the world. I don't approve of its expansion of bigger government or secularism. It has turned its back on God. He has been taken out of the schools. They want to take Him off the money, "In God we Trust". The churches have grown cold to the Holy Spirit. It is all about the feel good sensation we get on Sunday and that is supposed to last until next Sunday. We are not as Christians allowed worshiping in public functions. We have forgotten this country was founded on the principles of God.

Before seeking God this time around I fell into this secular world of Satan. My life consisted of a twelve pack of beer and a camp fire. I literally lived outside for a couple of years in an old camper in rural Morgan County, Tennessee near Wartburg. I thought I was pretty tough I guess but my standards had lowered to the point of a simple existence for my life. Yes, I worked a job and functioned as an undeclared alcoholic. I knew something was desperately wrong in my life. Once again sin had blinded me to my Friend. Are you blinded by sin? Won't you give Jesus an opportunity in your life?

It seemed like I lived in constant cold in the winter as I didn't even have heat one winter. Sometimes I would get excited about fixing the old camper up so I took the living floor out and then removed the front in order to seal up the drafts and make necessary repairs. Sometimes I would have critters just come on in a visit with me for a while. The field mice were very friendly. Then I threw a blue tarp over the top and that was the extent of the repairs. At least that kept the wind, rain and snow out to some degree.

I had no friends except drinking buddies. By this time my very existence on this earth was not for comfort and that twelve pack of beer a day was my master. Would you call the beer in my life an idol? My friends would tell me Smith you are drinking too much but they continued to drink with me. I really didn't need them anyway I had my beer and camp fire.

Then it happened even after going to jail a couple of times always related to drinking. The very last beer I drank was with my best friend. I'll just call him Frank and of course he knows who he is. For some unknown reason I got angry, can't even remember the reason, ha! I stormed out of the bar and began to drive home to my camper and I began to reach out to God once more. I decided life was not worth living. There was nothing left but to take my own life.

I don't know if I got lost again driving drunk but I called a friend for help. She knew I was drunk and of course she said and I'll never forget what she said. "You ole drunk, just go get some sleep". For those of you that have experienced anything remotely to this stupor, it made sense I could sleep it off and then kill myself in the morning.

I awoke the next morning and realized what I had almost done. The devil will lie, steal and convince you alcohol and drugs is okay and your life would not be near as much fun without these fiery darts the devil will use. He will kill and render your life in shambles. So close to Hell but God is good, just and full of Grace. A-Man

I fell to my knees and asked God to help me. My life was in shambles and I had no way to turn for I knew I could not do it on my own, Gods supernatural power of love looked down upon me and removed this addiction. When I got off my knees to this day I have never had the first desire to drink. I made a promise; my covenant with the Lord Once again my Friend, Jesus had rescued me from myself. My promise to my Friend was that I would never put strong drink to my lips again so long as I live. If in the future He saw this happening, please remove me from this earth that I might be with Him in Heaven, which is my covenant with Him. The devil lost that battle. To this day years later I have not drank or even had a desire to drink again. I was delivered from the addiction instantly. His grace is sufficient, Thank God, my Friend for salvation. This is nothing less than a miracle. Ask those who knew me then. Once again the ole man has been removed and the new man of Christ is present in my life. I am truly a new creature.

The war with the devil goes on as life becomes good. I still don't have many friends but I have no drinking buddies. I am a witness of Jesus Christ and have powerful testimonies that God brought me through. The test in each case has become my testimony. It is not about the life on earth now but it is preparing me for the coming of the Lord or will I meet Him in the sky someday? To serve Yahweh is my utmost desire. Either way my Friend Jesus is there for me and you. I urge you once again to trust in the Lord and make Him personal and your Friend. His spirit will enter your soul and your life will change. You will become the Sons and Daughters of God. We are all His children and He is calling a lot of us home to be with Him. I remind you age is not a factor for death here on earth. Don't put it off until it is too late. Eternity is forever. This life is but a whisper when you compare it in this concept. Accept Jesus and learn to live again.

It will remove drugs, alcohol, sexual perversions, pornography and sin. These are some of the pit falls leading up to and including divorce. No un-wanted pregnancies or abortions will be necessary. What have you got to lose? Seek God and He will find you and can repair the issues and prevent them from happening. Often the addiction is removed instantly and other repair comes later with His love and grace which He will provide in abundance. Let Him into your heart so the repair can begin today. Accept Christ as your personal savior and never look back on the ole man or woman of this world. Become renewed in Christ and receive your inheritance in Heaven. It is free to those who will but believe.

PICK UP YOUR CROSS

After "Repentance" you must pick-up your cross. This means old habits and ole friends must go. They will disappear from your life as this progression becomes your new life style. You have begun your first day in your quest and Test for eternity. This miracle and promise is a journey which will take us into the spiritual realm and place us in the Kingdom of Heaven.

It is a time to reach out to those like you. Put on your mask of Faith and breathe the pure oxygen of Christ. Your strength and endurance will come from the Holy Spirit sent from God. He is the endless supply of pure oxygen and the harvest fields are ready for the season.

Your brothers and sisters left behind will observe the new creature in you and will desire to follow you or become like you. But remember in order for your repentance, (the turnaround in your behavior) to be seen they can only absorb the over flow of your life. In John 7: 38 (NKJV) Christ says, "He who believes in me, as the scripture has said, out of his heart will Flow Rivers of living water." This simply means those who are satisfied by Jesus will themselves become channels of spiritual refreshment for others. The figure of Rivers contrasts with "a fountain", illustrating the difference between one's new birth and one's experience of the overflowing fullness of the Spirit-filled life.

I urge you to pick up your cross. Take responsibility to spread the gospel of Jesus Christ in whatever way God directs in your life. In the book of James, the brother of Christ, points out we are first fruits of God's creatures. He says the test of obedience is to become the doers of the Word and not just hearers. A great message is given in chapter 1 of James, verses 18-25 (NKJV); Of His own will He brought us forth by the word of truth, that we might be a kind of first fruits of His creatures. So then, my beloved brethren, let every man be swift to hear, slow to speak, slow to wrath; for the wrath of man does not produce the righteousness of God. Therefore lay aside all filthiness and overflow of wickedness, and receive with meekness the implanted word, which is able to save your souls. But be doers of the word, and not hearers only, deceiving your selves. For if anyone is a hearer of the word and not a doer, he is like a man observing his natural face in a mirror; for he observes himself, goes away, and immediately forgets what kind of man he was. But he who looks into the perfect law of liberty and continues in it, and is not a forgetful hearer but a doer of the work, this one will be blessed in what he does. The impartation of the Holy Ghost will provide power and direction in your life but it is the still small voice we must listen to.

To help the poor we must become rich not only in wealth but in spiritual gifts of the Father. Why would the poor reach out to someone that is poor also?

Our riches are not always measured in money or possessions. The Bible teaches us to be rich in the Love of Christ. We are to have no other Gods before us and to Love our neighbors as ourselves. We must love our brothers and sisters in Christ as we love ourselves.

To be a follower of Christ is a serious undertaking and bares with it the responsibility for regular Bible study and fellowship with others of the same accord. Yes, that means to attend a Spirit filled church and not to be a pew warmer but to take part, A-Man? In James 2, verse 26: (NKJV) for as the body without spirit is dead, so faith without works is dead also.

When you pick up your cross and walk away from the old habits and friends of the secular world it says I am no longer a friend to the world. The later part of verse 4 in James 4: (NKJV) says whoever therefore wants to be a friend of the world makes himself an enemy of God. In verse 7; therefore submit to God. Resist the devil and he will flee from you. That is a simple fix to most of the issues with sin if we will but do it. Submit to God and Resist the devil. These simple thoughts will repair all sin and stop in dead in its tracks.

As the new days walking in Christ and carrying the Cross shows you are now serious. The old habits will disappear and your friends left behind must be prayed for in order to save their soul. Not all people left behind were your friends and new friends will surface to lift you up and encourage you in your walk with Christ. This world of Jesus Christ, the Messiah, Yahshua of our life is one of excitement as we learn to do the will of the Father. The progressive life in Christ will bring joy, peace and love to the door step as you cross from the secular world to God. We are told to pray unceasingly not only for those left behind but for all things a new in our life. Stay in the Word and let God talk you through this choice to serve Him. Believe in God and His salvation through grace paid for by Jesus Christ. His shed blood and death on the cross as the Son of Man and Son of God paid the sin debt for all of mankind. His resurrection from the dead assures us He is truly the Son of God. Our religion is alive because Jesus lives.

By the grace of God we are saved through faith. It is not our good works or of ourselves, it is a free gift from God as mentioned in Ephesians 2: 8-10 (NKJV) for by grace you have been saved through faith, and that not of yourselves; it is the gift of God, not of works, lest anyone should boast, For we are His workmanship, created in Christ Jesus for good works, which God prepared beforehand that we should walk in them.

The apostle Paul wrote the book of Ephesians from a prison in Rome and here he is saying that we are saved because we believe in Christ and His resurrection much like the prisoner next to Christ believed as they both hung on crosses was saved just before His death. At this time the prisoner witnessed to the other prisoner also hanging from his cross saying this man has done nothing wrong and is not justified to die. And Jesus said in Luke 23: 43 (NKJV) "Assuredly, I say to you, today you will be with Me in Paradise."

In the book of James in chapter 2: verse 26 (NKJV) is saying we shall have works if we truly are spirit filled Christians and our body is both flesh and spirit: It would be impossible not to have works if you walk in the spirit daily. Your witness of Christ is part of the Great Commission to spread the gospel which we are all compelled to do. The prisoner which hung on the cross and was saved gave witness to the other prisoner that Jesus was not justified to die. Thus he was saved.

BY WORKS WE ARE NOT SAVED, BUT BY FAITH IN JESUS CHRIST AND THE GRACE OF GOD

As a child of God everything He has belongs to us. Therefore we are no longer a slave but a son or daughter, and if a son or a daughter then heir of God through Christ. The moment you were spiritually born into God's family, you were given some astounding birthday gifts: the family name, the family likeness, family privileges, family intimate access, and the family inheritance and all of the promises of God.

The New Testament gives great emphasis to our rich "inheritance." It tells us, My God will meet all your needs according to his glorious riches in Christ Jesus found in the book of Philippians 4: 19 (NKJV) and my God shall supply all your need according to His riches in glory by Christ Jesus. In eternity we will inherit even more. This will be a great home coming. We can fellowship with love ones, friends and get all those answers we have for God.

Paul said," I want you to realize what a rich and glorious inheritance He has given to His people". Ephesians 1: 18 (NKJV) the eyes of your understanding being enlightened; that you may know what is the hope of His calling, what are the riches of the glory of His inheritance in the saints. The eyes of your understanding being enlightened literally means that your heart may receive the brightness of hope resulting when the wealth of God's investment in you is understood.

HOLY GHOST SPIRIT: We all have access by one Spirit to the Father. The book of Acts explains the presence of the Holy Spirit received by the apostles. On the evening of His (Jesus) resurrection He came to the disciples in the upper room and breathed on them saying, the Spirit should come upon them mentioned in Acts 1: 8 (NKJV) but you shall receive power when the Holy Spirit has come upon you; and you shall be witnesses to Me in Jerusalem, and in all Judea and Samaria, and to the end of the earth.

On the day of Pentecost the Spirit came upon the whole body of believers in Acts 2: 1-4 (NKJV); When the Day of Pentecost had fully come, they were all with one accord in one place. And suddenly there came a sound from Heaven, as of a rushing mighty wind, and it filled the whole house where they were sitting. Then there appeared to them divided tongues, as of fire, and one sat upon each of them. And they were all filled with the Holy Spirit and began to speak with other tongues, as the Spirit gave them utterance.

Individual believers were for the first time baptized with the Holy Spirit into a unified spiritual orgasm likened to a body as Christ is the head. Pentecost is: fifty days. Originally a yearly Jewish celebration of harvest; also called the Feast of Weeks and the Feast of Harvest. On the first Pentecost after Christ's resurrection, the Holy Spirit uniquely came upon believers thus the Christian connection with Pentecost began here. Speaking in tongues besides the usual meaning of languages is to be guarded. The gift of tongues is a spiritual gift that comes with cautions and restrictions about its use. Speaking in tongues may refer to a foreign language or a unique utterance understood only by God or with His help as an interpreter.

Paul said in 1st Corinthians 14: 14 (NKJV) for if I pray in a tongue, my spirit prays, but my understanding is unfruitful. Verse 28 goes on to say; but if there is no interpreter, let him keep silent in church, and let him speak to himself and to God.

Verse 5 continues; I wish you all spoke with tongues, but even more that you prophesied; for he who prophesies is greater than he who speaks with tongues, unless indeed he interprets, that the church may receive edification. Paul simplify warns us of its use. It is better the church understand or be edified than to use tongues without an interpreter.

I have since childhood spoke with the utterance to God. It is a very solemn occasion and private between my Friend and I. It is when I am without words and this language will surface and truly is an utterance to God or it is straight from the heart and God knows the desires of my heart.

DON'T SUFFER THE VICTIM MENTALITY

Yes, I have turned my life around, now what? When I begin with my new walk it is going to be the same ole friends and their influence. It is going to be the same ole habits that took me down before and then I'm going to be right back in the same boat as before. I'll have the same ole spirit of lust and my desires will get me in trouble. I don't have a decent job and no one will help me. Life is always going to be against me. The only fun I know is drugs and alcohol. The only way for me to get money is to steal or deal in drugs.

I think it was Viktor Frank, who survived a Nazi death camp at Auschwitz, defined ultimate freedom as "the ability to choose ones attitude in any given set of circumstances, or to choose one's own way."

The worst prison in the world is the one we put ourselves in and we are captured by our MIND. A victim mentality cripples our ability to grow and strips us of the peace of God, which He has given us to live happy. This condition is a gradual deterioration that begins in childhood sometimes. You might have a low self-esteem and then this became the poor me complex. It could have been a love one that put you down. It could be from a series of wrong choices. Whatever the cause God has the fix for you. You can begin the change right now if you will take responsibility. No one can keep you in your current situation or frame of mind except you.

CHANGE IT TODAY

1. Begin to take responsibility. No one can keep you in your current situation, except you. Begin today to accept total responsibility to become a victor, not a victim.
2. Understand what responsibility means. The root word of "responsibility" is "response." You may not be able to control everything others do or say to you, but you can control your response. In your response lie your freedom and your growth!
3. Don't stay where you are. People may have had something to do with how you got into a certain situation, but only you can decide whether you stay in those circumstances or begin to live above them.
4. Stop the "victim" mentality. Begin to take full responsibility for your attitude and direction in life. We are given the choice of life and death so choose life and prosperity.
5. Ask the Holy Spirit to assist you. Taking full responsibility doesn't mean you're in it alone. God is with you always. His Holy Word will speak wisdom into your situation.

6. Don't quit or give away your power or let others decide for you. You have the choice to receive help from the Holy Spirit for recovery.

7. Take charge of what God has given you. The master said to the servant who hid his talent, "why didn't you at least invest it so I could have received interest?" He blamed the master and excused himself. As a result, he fell to the temptation of resentment and fear. He lost everything because he had a "victim mentality."

BE A GOOD STEWARD OF THE THINGS GOD HAS PROVIDED!
THINK IT AND SAY IT

No one can keep me down. I am not a victim. I am a victor. I take full responsibility for my responses in life—my attitudes and my decisions.

God has set before me prosperity or adversity. He has given me the power to choose. I choose prosperity!

Holy Spirit, I am asking for Your help. You live in me, and You are my Helper!

I refuse to give away my power by blaming others. I choose to respond to life with God's Word.

I take responsibility for my thoughts, my actions, and my reactions. I abandon the idea that my situation is the fault of anyone else.

Now that you have said it (verbalized) get into a real partnership with God. This is the only place where you cannot fail. Psalm 124 says that the Lord is on your side. This is not religion. This is common sense. You cannot fail when you awaken to the fact He walks with you and sticks closer than a brother.

Understanding is from God. Proverbs 3: 13-15 (NKJV); Happy is the man who finds wisdom, and the man who gains understanding; for her proceeds are better than the profits of silver and her gain than fine gold. She is more precious than rubies, and all the things you may desire cannot compare with her.

Start believing that it will work for you! It works for anyone. Remember what Jesus said in Mark 11; 23 (NKJV); For assuredly, I say to you, whoever says to this mountain, be removed and be cast into the sea, and does not doubt in his heart, but believes that those things he says will be done, he will have whatever he says. It only takes that grain of mustard seed faith.

CHAPTER 3

❧ ❧

IS A MEASURE OF FAITH ENOUGH?

Paul, the Apostle had been preaching as we are told, over twenty years the gospel of Jesus Christ when he wrote the Book of Romans. He at this time had not preached in Rome. I have been to Rome to view the sights of this ancient city. The Catacombs burials to this day are very sacred. (No Photos-when I was there)

True we are made in Gods image but our inability to earn favor with God is hampered with man's sin nature. We must live a pattern of life consistent with God's own righteousness.

We are all given a measure of faith according to Romans 12: verse 3; (NKJV) for I say, through the grace given to me, to everyone who is among you, not to think of himself more highly than he ought to think, but to think soberly, as God has dealt to each one a measure of faith. If you read on through 4-6 for as we have many members in one body, but all the members do not have the same function, so we being many, are one body in Christ, and individually members of one another, having then "gifts differing according to the grace that is given to us let us use them," etc.

What Paul is referring to is his own function in the body as an authoritative apostle through the grace given to him. The measure of faith is not saving faith but the faith to receive and to exercise the gifts God apportions to us. The "measure of faith" He (God) gives corresponds to the role He assigns as Creator and Redeemer. Our different gifts and abilities should make us love and depend more on one another, and therefore should make us more united as one body in Christ. It is through this mustard seed of faith that permits us to access the very throne room of Heaven. It is the difference between us and those that do not believe yet. We are the chosen ones to carry out the gospel of Jesus, "THE GREAT COMMISSION".

Paul is telling us to use the gifts received from God and accept this grace, directed by the Holy Spirit. Now I ask you how much faith you have. How much faith do you want? How righteous can you be? To increase your faith beyond the measure of faith given, you must show yourself worthy. The goal is to be more like Christ in this life. To seek His face and serve Him as Lord. I often ask God for more of His grace to increase my faith as I pray for my un-belief. For I know I have only a measure of faith and must depend on Jesus Christ. It is in my weakness He will manifest His strength through the Holy Ghost.

When you pray for someone to be healed ask God to use you as a willing vessel and manifest His healing power through you, for He is the great physician. It is not us as individuals that produce the healing it is through us. It is the supernatural power of God and His Holy Ghost Spirit that is real. Often you must be obedient to a request from God as He is using you as a willing vessel.

In 1st Corinthians 12: verse 4 (NKJV) says, there are diversities of gifts, but the same Spirit. If you read on Paul is telling us that these supernatural gifts are of God and not of man. It is not our heightened ability no matter how hard we try to copy what God has made available through the Holy Spirit. This becomes a reality when we walk on the Spirit, A-Man?

Verses 8-11 of this same chapter explain the nine gifts that made for a full manifestation of the Holy Spirit. For to one is given the word of wisdom, through the Spirit, to another the word of knowledge, through the same Spirit, to another, faith by the same Spirit, to another gifts of healings, by the same Spirit, to another prophecy , to another discerning of spirits, to another different kinds of tongues, to another the interpretation of tongues. But one and the same Spirit works all these things, distributing to each one individually as He wills.

The word of wisdom is a spiritual utterance at a given moment through the Spirit, supernaturally disclosing the mind, purpose, and way of God as applied to a specific situation. We will not even know sometimes why these thoughts are present. If it lines up with the Word of God it is from God.

The word of knowledge is a supernatural revelation of information pertaining to a person or an event, given for a specific purpose, usually having to do with an immediate need.

The gift of faith is a unique form of faith that goes beyond natural faith and saving faith. It supernaturally trusts and does not doubt with reference to the specific matters involved.

Gifts of healings are those healings that God performs supernaturally by the Spirit. The plural suggests that as there are many sicknesses and diseases, the gift is related to healings of many disorders. We are taught to anoint and lay hands on as we pray for these healings. It is through us as a willing vessel that God will perform.

The working of miracles is a manifestation of power beyond the ordinary course of natural law. It is a divine enablement to do something that could not be done naturally.

Prophecy is a divine disclosure of behalf of the Spirit, an edifying revelation of the Spirit for the moment, a sudden insight of the Spirit, prompting exhortation or comfort.

Discerning of spirits is the ability to discern the spirit world, and especially to detect the true source of circumstances or motives of people.

Different kinds of tongues are the gifts of speaking supernaturally in a language not know to the individual. This is not to be confused with the private utterance before God that we sometimes use when words are not present but God knows the desires of our heart. Paul speaks of his speaking in this Gods language.

The interpretation of tongues is the gift of rendering the Trans rational message of the Spirit meaningful to others when exercised in public. It is not the translation of a foreign language.

The gift of healing, is the church's mission. The clear intent is that the supernatural healing of the sick should be a permanent ministry of the church. This should go hand-in-hand with the Great Commission, which is the spreading of the gospel of Jesus Christ.

God is the eternal Spirit. He has no beginning or end. God is immortal and we are mortal. God is the Father of all creation, the

Creator of all. God exists in nature, but He is not nature, nor is He bound by nature. He is the Father, Son, and the Holy Spirit and is the fountainhead of Trinity. The Godhead exists of three Divine Persons each fully God.

What was once natural in the Garden of Eden is now referred as the Supernatural. Once before Adam and Eve ate of the forbidden tree, God would talk with them in the Garden. Through their disobedience and Satan's deceit sin entered their life.

Now it is considered supernatural when God speaks to you. The secular world has no understanding of the supernatural until they accept Christ and become born again.

HOW TO KNOW GODS WILL IN YOUR LIFE

1. The best way is to be familiar with the Bible. (Virtually everything we need to know concerning the will of God is in the Bible)

2. We must pray. This intimate communal conversation with God will teach you what pleases Him. The Bible says, "let the peace of God rule in your hearts," stated in Colossians 3: 15; (NKJV) and let the peace of God rule in your hearts, to which also you were called in one body; and be thankful. When His peace leaves you the inner turmoil immedi-

ately discovers you are going against God's will.

3. If you are unable to discern God's direction in your life say, Father, I want your will in my life above all else, please incorporate your plan and purpose for my life. He is faithful and just to answer and will direct your life.

4. Proverbs 3; 5-6; (NKJV) simply tells us to trust in the Lord with all your heart, and lean not on your own understanding; in all your ways acknowledge Him, and He shall direct your paths.

His ways of course is not our ways, no more than the Bible is fully understood. He would not be God if we understood Him and the Bible would not be a book of Divinity if it could be read and understood by man. The mystery of God is portrayed in the Holy Bible but I believe there is so much more to God than is revealed in His Holy Word. We are only mankind and were created for His pleasure.

GOD CAN AND WILL BRING HEALING TO YOUR BODY

While still in my childhood about the age of ten a lot of the kids in school had a disease of the scalp commonly called ring worm. You medically inclined have the proper name I'm sure. We boys just called it the mange with no regrets. This condition was a problem for us boys and of course the community. We even had radiation treatments not to mention that smelly salve we put on our heads after they shaved the hair off and to add insult to injury we slept in a skull cap, white of course. The final test would be when they would shine that ultra-violet light on our scalpe and sure enough if the critter was still active you could see the round circle glow under the light. Girls didn't seem to have it!

I heard someone talking about God and He could heal this infirmity why He could even raise the dead. Lots of people in the hills were healed just by asking God. I thought I was doomed to have ring worm and wear that stupid cap forever.

I was somewhat a loner as a child and I went to my Friend, God and asked Him to heal me. (In my spirit I hear preachers say now) He told me to hang my head out the window and let it rain on my head. Which I did being obedient as a child.

The next visit I had to the doctor for the light check the ring worm was gone. I didn't tell anyone for the longest time what God had done for me. He still directs my life and sometimes not in what would be considered a normal manner. Often there is an act of obedience we must do to receive the supernatural of the Father. I urge you to step out of what is normal and do what God is directing you.

If you have an issue with sickness or need a healing believe in your childlike faith that God will heal you. By your faith you will be healed. Is depression your devil? God can and will bring happiness to you and this simple fulfillment will bring joy to your very soul. Receive the fullness of Christ and follow Him. Remember sickness is from Satan. God does not desire any of us to be sick.

Is there a crisis in your life? If you will put God first and seek you first the Kingdom of God all things will be handed unto you. It is very simple to follow Christ. His load is light if you will but cast the burden to Him. The Bible tells us that by His strips we are healed and Jesus paid the price on that cross at Calvary.

I was on a mission trip in Sao Paula, Brazil helping to build a church. I was with the Baptist people this time as I go with different denominations. They certainly know how to get the job done. The New Hopewell Church of Knoxville and the Madison Avenue Church in

Maryville, TN. had partnered to erect a church in Sao Paula.

As the days went by my back had begun to really hurt. The herniation between L4 and L5 was acting up. This condition had the support of a MRI. I could hardly straighten up at the end of the day or walk without pain. You folks that have had this problem know what it is.

So I prayed the simplest prayer a man could pray and said, "Lord I am down here doing your work "Sir", if you will but take the pain away, you can give it back when the job is done". Months and years later my back has not hurt again except that which comes with getting older. God is more than capable and faithful to heal those that will only believe. He is real.

Incidentally the church in Brazil was being built in honor of an ole buddy of mine we called Derrick. At a camp fire many years ago on the French Broad River I gave the call that someone was being led into the ministry and it was Derrick. In my opinion he was the least likely since he had a slight speech impediment. He became a preacher and was a missionary in Sao Paula for 30 years or so. God is there on time all the time, A-Man?

I had not even seen Derrick for 50 years. The church is built now and this man of God is now retired. It is not ironic that God permitted me, in His time to see and know He truly allowed me to be fishers of men. Thank you my Friend Jesus, for the experience of Your promise. Yes, many years after that alter call He is faithful to those that wait.

God is in control even before we are born. He knows the number of hairs on our head. He knows when a sparrow falls dead to the ground. He can and will heal all your hurts and pains of this world in preparation for the reunion in Heaven. Our sickness and related pain is not of God but is through the devil. God is the great I AM. He is the Alpha and Omega. He is the beginning and the end. He is the great Physician. Without God there would be no life. He is life. It is His breath we operate in and yes I know He can raise the dead. Bring God in with all His glory into your life. Let Him rule and worship will be easy. God has not changed. He is the God of the past, present and future. Our test becomes our testimonies. He has the plan or formula for our life. It is not E=MC squared.

He will present you a plan for your life, the destiny each child of the universe searches for. Do you want Him to touch you so that the end of your dreams can be realized? Age is only a number. At this writing I have attained the age of 71 and at 60 I made my first sky-dive. You might ask why wait until that age? It is simply living out my childhood dreams and serving God. I am blessed with the health and attitude not only to live for God, my Friend I met so many years ago but to go forth with the Great Commission to the ends of the earth.

Whatever the mind can conceive as long as we make the right choices (God's Way) our life will be complete. We can be satisfied with God's promises. It is the conscience of our soul that will orchestrate the direction of our spirit. We will pay the consequences of those wrongful and sinful mistakes. If you want to make God laugh, just tell Him you are going to do it your way.

Sin is of course missing the mark of righteousness. Sin is the separator of prayers and their destination. It will interfere with our walk with God. Temptation is everywhere and the blinders for our path must be shielded by the armor of God.

In the fullness of Christ, possessing the Holy Spirit and walking in purity we will not be of this world but are bound by His desires. We are His hands and His voice led by the Word to serve just as Christ himself did. It is our responsibility and task to be a witness of His gospel.

In March 2009 God produced a miracle for this doubting Thomas attitude. What I am about to tell you some will have doubts and others will shout. As I share this testimony with you it started the previous year in the same place almost the same location. Is there a grid-way for doors and windows to Heaven?

On the previous trip to Dominica we were at the alter praying for people. There was a crowd of folks all around and in this situation I sometimes escape even closer to God. I asked God to show me a miracle. I was really praying for someone in particular to be healed.

To my surprise it rained on me in the church. I looked up and there were no water pipes or air-condition leaks and no one close enough to have slung sweat on me. In fact the water was cold as you would expect from rain. There was no sign of rain outside. I turned to my friend Dale and said, "Dale it has rained on me and he said I know I see the rain drops." May I remind you to be specific not only when you pray with supplication but be specific when you ask God for a miracle.

The next year almost to the foot in that same church meeting place God truly did produce a miracle healing for me to witness. I was on a pastor's convention with real preachers as I remind all I am not really a pulpit style preacher.

It all started the morning we were to bring the Word. Out of courtesy I'm sure I was asked if I wanted to bring the Word that morning. Of course I said yes to the opportunity to be a witness to my Lord and Friend of many years. I knew I could not be worthy in that capacity but felt led to do the best I could and I knew in my weakness God would take over. He truly did take over and produced more than one healing I'm sure.

That morning as I awoke before the two pastors I roomed with began to stir. I covered my head with the covers and wept to be used of God. There was no message in my mind and I had no idea what was about to happen. In faith I had accepted to do His will and it would have been so much easier to decline the offer to speak. My walk with Christ this go around, He gave me a new boldness through the Holy Spirit to be used by Him.

I began to speak through the interpreter and somewhere in to the message God just stopped me. I asked for the interpreter to bring Pastor John sitting on the front row. I asked him to anoint me with oil. Pastor John a native to Dominica was in his nineties I'm sure and I had never seen anyone with the faith he possessed. When he was drunk in the spirit I expected him to fall at any time but he never did.

We must be obedient to the unction to the Holy Ghost and the Spirit told me to ask for a double portion of what I had seen in Pastor John. As he made his way slowly up I began to pray for the release of the Holy Ghost in the church.

Pastor John began to pour the anointing oil on my head and my first thought was the new suit I had on, ha! He did not stop with a drop or two but it seemed like he poured the

whole bottle on my head. The power of God
began to force me down to the concrete and I
literally felt like I was being shoved in to the
floor.

Pastor John stopped and the Spirit said to
give him my trusty pocket knife. The Bible I
use to this day I traded a pocket knife for.

I stopped the service and through the interpreter asked if the church had issues with
health, or any sickness, or any satanic presence to come forth and let me pray for them.
It looked like the whole church was coming
forward.

The very first man I prayed for pulled his
collar back to show me what looked like a
tumor, about the size of an orange in the neck-
shoulder region. He said in broken English he
had a sickness in his neck. So I un-screwed
the cap of my little bottle of anointing oil and
felt so insecure that I said Jesus be there for
me. I said Lord you know I cannot do this
alone.

I began to pray and plead the condition
of my heart, as I stretched forth the bottle of
anointing oil and touched the tumor with my
other hand. The Spirit said, "rub-it". As I began
to rub it I prayed these words Lord Manifest
your healing power through me your willing
vessel. For you are the Great Physician.

Suddenly the tumor began to get smaller
and smaller, down to a very small lump and
the Spirit said to rub it also, so I did. The tumor

was removed. My Friend, Jesus came through for me again. I'll never be a doubting Thomas again. By the way my name is Thomas.

I don't know who was more surprised by the healing the man healed or me. To God be the glory. My praise is to the Father. Many people were healed and I know God used me in the service of course I began to walk in the Spirit and TIME stood style.

If I ever had any doubts in God or His power it is now removed.

There was a young girl the brothers brought to me and said she has a demon. I anointed her and she seem to fly backwards with a mighty force. As she lay on the concrete on her back the cries of the demonic spirits came out of her as she wiggled and screamed. We held her down to keep her from hurting herself. Four men were holding her down, one to each limb. It was all I could do to hold the one wrist down with my two hundred pound frame.

As I rebuked the devil in no other name than Jesus and pleaded His blood over the young girl, her strengthen resistance was over whelming. She weighed maybe ninety pounds. This went on for several minutes and at one point I released her wrist as she got very still. Instantly she pulled a hand full of her hair out by the roots. So we continued to pin her to the concrete...

Then a woman came and stood over her and rebuked the devil and commanded it to leave her body and she became still. She had a peace about her as we helped her to the bench seat. Laura then began to give her the agape, love of God she so desperately needed. The next day I saw her with her hands held high in the surrender position as she jumped up and down before the Lord.

My walk with the Lord brings Him even closer as a Friend in Jesus of long ago. As you read these words learn by my mistakes and seek God until He finds you. I only rest or pause between mission trips; not tired of course but just knowing when and where God would use me again to do His will.

I'm sure many more miracles took place that day. My sense or presence of being was distorted as God used me as a willing vessel. To God be the glory.

OFTEN OUR MIRACLE REQUEST MADE IS FOLLOWED BY AN INSTRUCTON FROM GOD

This instruction will be a direct connection to "OBEDIENCE". It is not signs or wonders or even a conformation. It is simply faith.

Know that God has heard the request and be still. Listen to what the Holy Spirit is saying. How many have seen or had miracles happen in their life? A few years ago my daughter was scheduled for a heart exam. She had taken the steps necessary to justify a further exam at the hospital. She was young for this I thought but they said it had to be done and all of her test up to this point had been done.

The night before, I was at a tent revival in Maryville, Tn. The group was of the Dave Hogan Ministry serving in the rural country side of Mexico. There were several documented cases of the dead being raised in their ministry. As I listened to the awesome testimonies I saw a young man coming down the aisle praying for people. As he came closer I thought why not ask him to pray over a little bottle of anointing oil and use it to anoint my daughter the next morning.

So I stepped out in Faith and stopped him. I ask if he would pray over the anointing oil. As he touched my hands that were holding the oil the power of God literally knocked me to the concrete floor. All I can remember was he was speaking in tongues and then I could hear the metal folding chairs clanging on the concrete. The next thing I got to my knees, then a chair, and I was exhausted. The power of God is so awesome. Don't put God in a box and say he can help my headache but raise the dead.

I tell you all of this to finish my story. The next day at the hospital we had a word of prayer for Teresa and as they began to roll her away. I stopped them and said, "I must anoint her and pray again." As I applied the oil to her forehead big puppy dog tears rolled down her checks. They took her away and it seemed like eternity but in just a few minutes the doctor returned. His comment was I don't understand there is nothing wrong. Hallelujah!

In the recovery room as I talked with my daughter she said, "Daddy, I knew when you touched me I was healed." Was it in the oil? No, it was in the faith and obedience.

You will have to agree this is a long ways from the mountains of W. Va. But Jesus is still my friend. He can be your friend too if you will but believe that He is the Son of God. That He died for us and arose again defeating death. He will accept you just as you are. Salvation is free and the joy is indescribable and eternity is forever. I urge you to come aboard.

God does not always call the qualified but He certainly qualifies those He calls. Remember He knows your heart and rivers of living water will flow from your belly or heart mentioned in John 7: 38 (NKJV) "He who believes in Me, as the Scripture has said, out of his heart will flow rivers of living water." Those that are truly satisfied by Jesus will themselves become channels of spiritual refreshments for others. This is the overflowing fullness of the Spirit-filled life.

Knowing that God is real and searching for His approval will lead you to a new dimension. We know Moses brought forth the Ten Commandments. We know we now live under the Grace of God and Salvation of Jesus Christ. We are told to just believe and repent our sins but I say do not disregard the teachings in the Old Testament for here lies the beginning of God, as Yahshua fulfilled the teachings of the Old Testament.

GOD REVEAL AND CONNECT OUR NATURAL SENSES TO YOUR HOLY PRESENCE

Oh Lord, our Father in Heaven as twilight appears let this be the day you reveal your Holy Presence. Excite our human senses to recognize your Holy Spirit. It is this direction we need to function and to do thy will. Position your angels in our life that they might not only protect us but beckon us to Your Call here on earth. Lord at this stage of life we are merely mortals encompassed in this human body. Our soul and spirit person needs to be able to separate from the flesh and come into a direct relationship with power from the Holy Spirit.

Allow our senses to be used by the spiritual man in a way that we have direct communication with the Father and know by the sound of His voice to be obedient to the Holy Ghost. When we leave the mortal body and venture into the Will of the Father it is only to bring glory to God and Praise to His Name. To become a follower of Yahshua, the Son of Man and the Son of God is only possible if we know the voice of God, Yahweh.

Let us be bold and take up our seat of power positioned in advance that we might be used in His plan of Salvation. The gospel must be spread through the world before His second coming. We are one with the Spirit in our walk with the messiah, Jesus. Give us the gift of Spiritual discernment to be able to see within the realm of the supernatural. Let us Oh Lord, be able to connect our eyes to the eyes of God, and see the things which aren't as though they are. Let us connect our vision with His vision that our lives may become more intimate with His will. It is not about us, but about the Father we pray, as our very soul searches for His Holy presence. Your will be done on earth as in the Kingdom of Heaven.

As we find others in this walk here on earth that You, Oh Father God, have a desire to touch, join our hearts that they might come to know you. Our vision is limited except through the power of God. Our connection is the mustard seed of faith that can move mountains. This must be enough Lord for us to build on, as the level of expectancy develops into total control given to Your Will.

We must keep sight of the vision of prayer for our communication is found here in your love. Be still and know that You are God is the other portion of our prayer life that completes the conversation with You, Abba Father. Allow our obedience to be acceptable as You guide us to do the will of the Father.

It is not enough Oh Lord, for Your presence, but we seek a touch from Your finger that will enable Your power to flow through this mortal body. Allow the healing flow of health manifest within us that a simple touch encompasses the tangible and transferable power of healing. We know that sickness is of the devil and that Satan has come to steal, kill and take away a fruitful life. Dear God, your breath brought life to our bodies, make a way that this mortal body be used as a willing vessel to do thy will. Keep us sensitive to Your presence that we might know how to be obedient. As we approach these final days on earth let Your praise be heard as, "well done my faithful servant."

As we follow the Holy Scriptures that explain your healing powers allow us to pray them with confidence that the Holy Spirit will act upon them and "yes", Lord we pray this in the name of Jesus. Jesus paid the price as the ultimate sacrifice on the cross at Calvary. By His strips we are healed. His death was for us and all mankind that our sins are forgiven and we are healed by His strips. Eternity, our very salvation, is free and the debt is paid in full. His resurrection defeated death and proves He is truly the Messiah, the Son of God.

May Your cloud of Glory cover us with Your Holy Presence and allow the sweet smell of God to fill our nostrils. Take us to that place of Divine worship in the Heavens. Give us a new body that knows no sickness and unite us with those love ones that serve you now. Your grace is abundant to deal with us in this human state, but we repent daily that you might know our shame and imperfections. To the God that knows even when a sparrow falls to the ground forgive us of our transgressions and sinful nature.

May we taste life as a modern day disciple and spend eternity with You, Oh Lord. Assist us with those decisions which balance the scale from right or wrong. Give us to do good and right as we cast out evil. Give us to love as we cast out hate. Give us to wisdom as we cast out doubt and un-belief. We pray for our un-belief in the attack brought forth by the prince of principalities.

How sweet the savor as our soul touches through the Spirit in communion with thee my God. It is my pleasure to taste the fruit found only in Your perfection. May we walk with Thee in the Garden of Eden? Make Yourself present in our life.

Once again, my Lord forgive me of my transgression, inequities and un-confessed sin in my life. Go past my life and see into my heart. Find me worthy I pray for favor in this life that I might live for You. Search my soul for the imperfections to remove and replace them with righteousness and purity. Bring the miracle fire that un-holiness in my heart be set free and not held captive by sin. Allow me Oh Lord, to share my love for you that my walk will win others to Christ that their soul may not burn in Hell.

Separate us from ourselves. Allow the spirit man in me to claim dominance over my soul.

With this separation allow me to claim the DNA of Christ. Those that have lost this DNA because Satan has taken from you what God put in your life. Step forward in repentance. Place sincerity foremost in our heart and through the grace of God replace this back-slidden condition. Surrender your existence and allow the pressures that surround you be removed. Restore my Lord, the self-esteem and repair my guilt and know a new beginning is on the horizon when morning comes.

It is always better to want something you don't have than to want something you don't need. When you cannot see what tomorrow holds don't make hasty decisions. When you don't know what to do, then do nothing, wait on the Lord. Into every life comes a dark season where you have to let the Lord accomplish His work. It might be only a test or trial but we are told to wait on the Lord and in His time we will have the desires of our heart, for His ways are not our ways.

When you find yourself in a dark place allow the assurance of salvation shine the light to guide your footsteps. With this salvation comes the light of Christ. Allow it to guide your path. The footsteps have just created your path and as you look back on yesterday your trail will reveal a highway that God has prepared. It is this darkness where God will reveal to you His way. In the Book of Psalm chapter 30, verse 5 (NKJV) tells us for

His anger is but for a moment, His favor is for life; weeping may endure for a night, but joy comes in the morning.

Stay where you are and the Lord will show you the way. Things in our life must die in order for God to bring completions and re-birth. He will shut doors but not until the other doors are open.

Daily repentance and renewal of our mind allows God to purify our heart soul and spirit. Your faith will not lead you astray.

DON'T LIMIT GOD

Don't limit God in your pursuit to live a Christian life or to be a follower of Christ. Saturate your body with the Holy Spirit and know that His touch will release the very power of God.

When you plant a garden you invest in the seed. It is the same garden of desire with God. Your desire is to serve and please our Lord and will bring forth a mighty harvest. Our seed is to be a witness. Sometimes we plant the seed and sometimes we are involved in the harvest. This task God will show to us.

Fertilize the soil with the Holy Spirit and all the nutrients will be present. It is through prayer and supplication that God will produce the favorable weather with rain and sunshine. The rain will come in due season keeping the roots supplied with water.

This paints a picture of life on earth and awaiting the return of the Messiah. Our soul must be enriched by the presence of the Holy Spirit. We are told to produce fruit and feed those less fortunate. We are told to share the gospel of Jesus Christ with all creatures. It is through the Holy Spirit and the study of the Word which guides us through this journey.

If the weeds in your garden have over taken the harvest it will affect the "first fruits" demanded by Yahweh. The weeds will be removed when sin is eliminated. The crucifixion of the Messiah paves the way of those sins are forgiven. Our sin debt has been paid in full for all mankind. Remove the (weeds) of sin in your life and repent. Don't put-off removing the (weeds) of your life. The bondage of sin will choke out the harvest.

His shed blood on the cross is more than sufficient to usher in the supernatural redeeming salvation that will save our soul. We are bought with a price as Yahweh sent His Son as the perfect sacrifice to die for all mankind. When the storms of life and bad weather come it is the "Son-shine" that will bring fulfillment and satisfaction back.

It is the spoil of life and not the soil of life, which we came from as mentioned in Genesis 1: 7; (NKJV) and the Lord God formed man of the dust of the ground, and breathed into his nostrils the breath of life; and man became a living being. The "spoil of life" manifest Sin into existence which is a signal of wrong doing. Our conscience sends the alarm and with the God given choice we decide to take the road of righteousness or follow Satan down the river of wrong choices to the lake of Hell. There are many souls incarcerated by wrong choices. These imperfections are amplified by the habits of our life. It is the wrong choice only one time that will become the habit that will become the hidden sin we all must repent of.

God will make a way for us to seal in His goodness if you will but open the door of repentance. His grace is more than sufficient to extend mercy if you will but ask. Don't battle in the realm of doubt for we are told that Satan is the prince of principalities and is ever present as a fallen angel. If you are not sure where you stand in this battle, then you are not standing at all. We must arm ourselves as mentioned in Ephesians 6: 10, to take up the whole armor of God.—I urge you to read this in its entirety. Claim this teaching in its true state and proclaim it before Satan.

Has your life been less than acceptable to enter a pure and holy existence? Is your walk with Christ been one of uncertainty one day and the next one you feel His very touch? If this is the case you are not walking in the Spirit. Every day should be a testimony of righteousness required to dwell in the Spirit. The borders of life determine your direction. Don't walk the fence of doubt. Make a decision for Christ. Allow stability and balance to lead you to this righteousness. Let Heaven be your destination and your choice be with the Messiah. Change your mind and change your life. Christ is the only way to the Father. Invite the Holy Spirit to dwell in you. All power in Heaven and Earth are in those which receive and allow Him to inhabit their flesh and soul. Pray for the spiritual gifts which are the inheritance of those that accept and believe in Yahshua, the Messiah. We are told and instructed of these gifts in 1ˢᵗ Corinthians

12: 7-10 (NKJV); but the manifestation of the Spirit is given to each one for the profit of all: for to one is given the word of wisdom, through the Spirit, to another the word of knowledge, through the same Spirit, to another, faith, by the same Spirit, to another gifts of healings, by the same Spirit, to another the working of miracles, to another, prophecy, to another, discerning of spirits, to another different kinds of tongues, to another the interpretation of tongues.

We have been given the power to cast out demons but before we worry about the thorn in our brothers eye let us remove the object in our own eye. It is important to examine our own life and listen to the conscience of the soul to be aware of those things which hamper our walk in "The Spirit". We must repent daily asking God to remove the sins of imperfection and to remove also those hidden sins covered by habits of the flesh. Sin is the missing of the mark and is the evidence of the "spoil in our life". It is this very evidence that God will judge your entrance to eternity. Jesus can repair your life and remove the destination of Hell.

Know who you are in Christ and accept the position of authority and simply proclaim the gospel of Christ. Understanding will come to those that receive, through the power of the Holy Spirit they will take up his or her cross in the battle against Satan. Isaiah 43: 2; (NKJV) says when you pass through the waters, I will be with you; and through the rivers, they shall not overflow you. When you walk through the fire, you shall not be burned. Nor shall the flame scorch you.

When you are called to be a pastor the standards of your responsibility must change. It is no longer your life you must account for but the flock of sheep assign to you. They must know your voice and must feel your love. You must be there for them. When they call, it is an opportunity to "feed my sheep". Some of your sheep are in the lamb or kid stage and are babes in Christ, while others have become the elders of the church. Their diets range from milk to meat, A-Man? Some will join you in the ministry and will hold your hands up like Aaron did for Moses.

As your flock grows and more are fed meat (the Word of God) the battle is won for the mighty army of God. The battle is won as people change from the infant stage to mature men and women in Christ. As your flock increases look for the spiritual leaders using Spiritual discernment. If they are not willing to accept normal for their praise and worship and seem a little fanatic (a fan of) for Christ, they are ready to claim their position of authority. As more and more of your flock are directed by the Holy Ghost it is time to plant another church to attract more sheep. To spread the great commission is our commandment. Be counted in last days as one that trust in the Lord.

If Moses had not trusted in God would God have used him? Would he have seen the "burning bush" and known that he was on Holy Ground? Would God have used him to part the red sea? As a messenger of God, Moses was told to warn pharaoh to let His people go out of bondage or many plagues would come upon Egypt. God used Moses to lead his people in the wilderness for forty years. God will complete His course in His time and not ours......

God will lead the way for believers that have the faith of our fathers. He is not a respecter of persons. He will use you as a willing vessel if you will become obedient to the unction of the Holy Ghost. It is the right time to step out and serve the Lord, Jehovah in these last days.

Exodus 13: 21, (NKJV) tells us, and the Lord went before them by day in a pillar of a cloud to lead the way; and by night in a pillar of fire, to give them light, so as to go by day and night.

DON'T DRAG YOUR PAST
INTO TOMORROW

When God forgives your sin, don't take it with you into tomorrow. Lay your sins, worries, doubts, and trust at the Cross of Jesus. It is the witness of salvation in His plan that these sins be given to Him. His death and resurrection on that cross paid this sin debt. If you take the past with you into tomorrow it manifests your un-belief. You must know your sins are forgiven.

We are called to be a witness of this salvation Jesus brought to us in God's plan, to remove and forgive sin in our life. It is our walk with God to come closer to Him and to seek the face of Jesus Christ. This simply means to become more like Him. He is our example to live by. The Holy Bible is not only our guide book but the divine Word of God. It will bring focus to our walk in this life.

I seek to live each day in the "now time", not wanting the past or the future. As I remember time gone by for the writing of this book it allows me to detach myself from the past and appreciate the "now time". It is this day and this day only that is important to me, for this is my new day in Christ. I truly became a new creature in Christ.

If you drag your past with you, this gives the devil the thoughts, temptations, old habits, baggage, etc. to remind you of all the fun you use to have; this contact with the past known by the devil will bring division in your life and successfully separate us from God once again. We must remain aware of the tricks he will use against us. Satan is a worthy foe and is a fallen angel and knows the Bible also. The fun we use to have will not compare to what God has in store for us. We are grafted in to His chosen people. All of the blessings are manifested to us and the joy, love, and peace will take on a new meaning for our lives.

You do not have to be present in a church to accept this. There doesn't have to be church music or a preacher doing his thing. All that is necessary is to sincerely ask God to forgive you of your sins. As you repent, accept Christ as the living Son of God and believe His death and resurrection on that third day paid your sin debt in full. Read John 3: 16 for your assurance from the divine Word of God. (NKJV) "For God so loved the world that He gave His only begotten Son, that whoever believes in Him should not perish but have everlasting life."

If you will diligently search for God, He will find you. He did not go away, we did. We are all born into sin and it is the bondage of sin that separates us from God. He will never leave you or forsake you and will stick closer than a friend. Just believe and join with the followers of Christ, A-Man.

No sin is little therefore we should concentrate our efforts to be sinless, holy, and pure In God's eyes. This is not an easy mission and only through the power of the Holy Spirit can we attain this goal. If Satan can manipulate your thoughts he can capture your mind. Be reminded that the battle ground is in your mind.

Paul, the apostle said less of me Lord and more of You. It is through praise and worship we approach the throne room. Battles are won when we thank Him for the situation we are in. In this realm of thought we have just invoked spiritual warfare and God has never lost a battle.

It is so awesome to walk in the Spirit and know God is at our very finger tips. When in the Spirit you won't have to call someone to pray for you or you won't have to call 911. All you have to do is call upon God.

That tiny light at the end of the tunnel can become the center point of your life if you will make that light be the Light from God. It will magnify within you and His brilliance will shine that no jewel can match and its luster cannot be contained.

Most of our battles are nothing more than spiritual warfare manifest in us through the image of our minds. This imagination is the focal point that will control our choice between good and evil. Satan will use our past to cause chaos to convince us that you have failed or what is the use in trying. Does this sound familiar? If the devil can manipulate your thoughts you will fall back into the sin trap.

Use all forces made available including angels from Heaven. Pray for the hedge of protection around us. Ware the entire armor of God found in Ephesians chapter six. In the stillness of the night let us dwell under your wing, Oh Lord. Hide us from the evil one that brings diversity to hamper us in life. Help us in our test that they might become our testimonies.

Help us not to be lulled to sleep because of our good reputation or self-righteous attitude. This very complacency may take you to Hell-not a curse word, but a real place. Let us constantly examine ourselves before the Lord, asking Him to enlighten our hearts to any un-acknowledged sin and to cleanse us, removing all satanic or demonic force from our presence. Yes, demons still operate here in the United States for those of you that do not operate in the spiritual realm. Jesus said we have all power to cast out demons. Do you have enough faith? If the Bible says it let us accept it as the truth and Holy Word of God.

GENERATIONAL CURSES

As God spoke to me this morning I am reminded of Isaiah 53: 4-5 (NKJV) Surely He has borne our grief's, and carried our sorrows; yet we esteemed Him stricken, smitten by God, and afflicted. Verse 5, says but He was wounded for our transgressions. He was bruised for our iniquities; the chastisement for our peace was upon Him, and by His stripes we are healed.

Our healings are both physical as well as mental. The sins of our fathers handed down from father to son or daughter is not only a repeat of history it becomes generational in nature. It becomes a generational curse. This can be transferred and re-lived over and over until the curse is broken. These afflictions can come from our ancestors unknown to us and long since forgotten in time. The words "grief and sorrow" from verse four in Hebrew, specifically mean physical affliction. These curses can appear as physical sickness or mental anguish. Your very nature can appear as one of constant mistakes brought about by wrong decisions or choices. These choices tend to reappear and be the wrong choice over and over until we accept it as nothing more than "who we are". And this is not who we are but a satanic influence handed down from one generation to the next. We are held in bondage by a curse we might not be aware of.

The words "borne and carried" refer to Jesus' atoning work on the cross. In Matthew 8: 17 (NKJV) says, that it might be fulfilled which was spoken by Isaiah the prophet, saying: "He Himself took our infirmities and bore our sicknesses." It is these words that link the grounds of provision for both our salvation and our healing to the atoning work of Calvary. Neither salvation nor healing is automatic but it must be received by faith.

These "curses" can be reversed. The power of the Holy Ghost lives within us as believers and followers of Christ. Jesus the Son of God was sent to Calvary as the ultimate sacrifice, sinless and without blame so that the Word could become completed spoken of in Isaiah. We are His "seed" as the redeemed in Christ. The Blood of Christ is purification needed to remove our sins, transgressions, and inequities as well as curses. It is through the atonement of Christ and His shed blood that we can claim all "generational curses" be removed in His Holy name.

Within your heart and all sincerity through faith ask Jesus to rebuke Satan in your life. Repent of all sin in your life spoken and hidden. Rebuke Satan in your life and proclaim you are no longer held captive by the bondage of a generational curse. Plead the blood of the Messiah to wipe away this yoke of your ancestors. Exercise the power of the tongue and make these words known to

Satan that through your Holy Ghost power we claim dominion over the curses placed upon us. Jesus remove this curse from me and my family. I accept this action in faith and know in my heart my life is free to serve thee. Enrich my soul with your Light so that others may know salvation is free. Eternity is forever with your promise of Heaven. We thank you and praise you and all glory belongs to You, Father God.

Numbers 14: 18 (NKJV) says, The Lord is longsuffering and abundant in mercy, for giving iniquity and transgression; but He by no means clears the guilty, visiting the iniquity of the fathers on the children to the third and fourth generation.

This text is taken from the Old Testament referred to as the Law. The Law is anointed by the Word of God, but God sent His Son, Jesus, the Messiah, to fulfill the Law. As followers of Christ we are not under the Law per say. Yes, we are grafted into the chosen Jewish people and have accepted Christ, the Messiah. Jesus came to fulfill the Law. This allows His death and resurrection to become the corner stone and acceptance that makes possible the forgiveness or clearing of our request for removal of the "Generational curse" of our fathers.....

Galatians 3: 13 (NKJV) says, Christ has redeemed us from the curse of the Law, having become a curse for us, (for it is written, "Cursed is everyone who hangs on a tree")

Now let us read from verse 10-14. For as many as are of the works of the Law are under the curse; for it is written, "cursed is everyone who does not continue in all things which are written in the book of the Law, to do them." But that no one is justified by the Law in the sight of God is evident, for "the just shall live by faith."

Yet the Law is not of faith, but the man who does them shall live by them. Christ has redeemed us from the curse of the Law, having become a curse for us (for it is written. "Cursed is everyone who hangs of a tree") and finally in verse 14 it says that the blessing of Abraham might come upon the Gentiles in Christ Jesus, that we might receive the promise of the Spirit through Faith. A-Man and A-Man.......

CHAPTER 4

❧ ❧

CAST RELIGION OUT THE DOOR

On a recent trip to Cleveland, Tn. we attended a TL Lowery healing, teaching, seminar or conference. I can say this without reservation the work book on healing is in itself an encyclopedia on healing. It truly is anointed and will not only build your trust in Christ but enable you to know God will and does heal. It is not His will for us to be sick and Jesus Christ has paid the price at Calvary. I thank you Brother Lowery for laying hands on each of us in attendance. Many were healed and others like me have a burning desire for a double portion of faith. You followers of Christ know what I mean by this. There were some two hundred or more in attendance and the Holy Ghost flowed so freely. It is an awesome experience to be in the presence of God and to fellowship with saints. I know everyone there took something home with them to build

upon. There were many denominations represented in the auditorium and we were all of
the same accord just like in the upper room
mentioned in the Book of Acts.

The presence of the Lord was there and as
I stood waiting my turn in line to receive my
blessing from the man of God, butterflies had
taken over and my knees were shaking and
trembling. My prayer was Oh Lord; allow the
religions present to go out the door into the
parking lot. It is not about the denomination
or choice of worship you have but it is simply
the spiritual person being released to function when the glory cloud of God is present. If
you have ever received the Holy Ghost or been
slain under the Spirit as some will call it, your
anticipation will heighten.

I stepped forward and told the men of God
I wasn't there to ask for healing but that I
needed a double portion of faith needed for
the many mission fields that God was sending
me. Dr. Lowery, with his baritone voice took
my wrist and said, in a loud voice, "Stand on
your tiptoes and surrender to Heaven (reach
up)." As we began to pray I could hear no more
words. In fact, I am at a loss to know exactly
what happened.

I lay on the floor in the fetal position and
trembled with the Holy Ghost power. I literally
felt like a horse had kicked me in the stomach
and I knew this was real. Thank you Lord for

this promotion from faith to faith. Enable me to do thy will and bring glory to the Kingdom.

People, when you come to the realization God is real, religion goes out the door. When you not only feel His Holy presence but know He is there for you individually only tears of gratitude can begin to show your return love. People for centuries have come to know God. Each one in their own way on Gods calling and the void in your heart is filled with His love and grace. Now God will communicate with you as a child of God. God will answer your curiosity and direct your every footstep if you will but learn to hear His voice. "For my sheep will know my voice"

The walk with God will become more special as you experience life and increase in age. It is through the Holy Spirit that we can tap into the gifts of the Spirit mentioned in 1st Corinthians 12. The Spiritual gifts through the Holy Ghost can manifest wisdom, knowledge, faith, healing, the working of miracles, prophecy, discernment, speaking in tongues and interpretation of tongues.

The way of the cross has been made simple, through grace as we receive salvation. Your salvation will usher you into His Holy presence. This is a free gift from God and all that is required is to repent, accept Jesus, (Yahusha) believe He is the Son of God, died and arose on the third day. The word repent means to change your mind. If you struggle here in understanding you must visualize through faith, the blood of Christ as He hung on that cross until death. This blood is our sacrifice to God through Jesus, His Son. Christ is our sacrifice for the many sins in our life. He died for all of mankind.

You are forgiven and all sins and short comings are as white as snow in God's eyes. Jesus was sent there to be the ultimate sacrifice and fulfill the Old Testament of God's Word. As we search for God until He finds us it is through this special porthole and season we gain fellowship. This communication always in prayer and supplication can take you into His area of Holiness. This must be done without sin in your life and without aught with your neighbor. It is here you can receive a glimpse of His power and love. It is nothing like the love we find on earth from a spouse, child, friend or parent. When His presence is known or felt the obsidian of darkness will become the whitest white our eyes can behold. It is here a change will occur. To be touched by the love of God is indescribable. We must practice praise and worship for it is here we are brought into His presence. His agape Love is indescribable.

BE READY UNTO WEARING OF YOUR GARMENTS, JESUS IS COMING SOON

Lest you will walk naked when Christ comes......Revelation 16: 15 (NKJV); "Behold, I am coming as a thief. Blessed is he who watches, and keeps his garments, lest he walks naked and they see his shame."

To have (garments rather than be naked) relates to spiritual preparedness or readiness. This readiness begins first in your mind and continues into the Word of the Bible. We must be ready in the twinkle of an eye to meet Him. This means our mind, our imagination, our habits, and desires need to be holy and pure. Don't embarrass yourself with the shame of Sin which is naked before God anyway. Walk up-right and guiltless before the Lord.

Eliminate evil that lurks within, searching the heart by the darkness of the soul, but use the Light of God known as our conscience. One small illumination of a candle will dissipate the darkness it touches. In Ephesians 6 we are given the clothes necessary for our protection. These are spiritual garments adorned for protection from those fiery darts of Satan.

The root of evil is enslavement and the degradation of the human spirit. Each human being is the image of God without our sin. Liberation from bondage and freedom can transcend the shackles of sin and become free. It is our mindset that emerges in the context of a relationship with the Divine. Therefore remove the shackles of sin and experience the love, joy and peace which are the highest form of excitement. Thus your life shall become one of a natural high without drugs, alcohol, or sex.

Cleansing of the soul is necessary to retain your freedom. This is a daily repentance of sin as sin will prevent your communication with God, which is the source of power to live this life style. Communal prayer is our connection and it must be one of intimacy. Don't be repetitive but slow down, ponder your words, (write them down, if it helps) and show God your sincerity in this special time with Him.

Your puffiness of self or self-righteousness or holier than thou attitude must be buried with the rags of uncleanliness. Our spiritual wellness begins when we accept God for His Holy and virtual power and with fear and admiration of His awesome power. Sometimes only God Seekers ever experience the magnitude of Gods power. Do you want to become the new generation of God Seekers?

In Ephesians 6: 10, (NKJV); Says, finally, my brethren, be strong in the Lord and in the power of His might.

I like what was said right out of my study Bible. Finally may be rendered "from now on" or henceforth. The spiritual battles we are engaged in exist "from now on" until the Lord's return. There is no cease fire or truce this is an all-out war with the enemy, the devil.

Maybe the power of God ought to never be taken lightly. He spoke the world into existence and He can speak it out of memory.

Verse 11 tells us to put on the whole armor of God, that ye may be able to stand against the wiles of the devil....The Greek phrase "put on" denotes a sense of urgency, demanding immediate action.—"to stand" has military overtones with its Greek meaning to resist the enemy and hold a critical position in battle.—The wiles of the devil is simply Satan and his strategy, schemes and tactics against believers.

Verse 12 warns us...For we wrestle not against flesh and blood, but against principalities, against powers, against the rulers of the darkness of this world, against spiritual wickedness in high places.

A lot of activities in the Bible may involve demons. Often they cause physical disease or mental suffering. Of course not all mental disorders are demonic in origin. Demons are known to tempt people into immoral practices using the weakness of our flesh. Some people can be possessed by demons although demons are committed to do evil. Demons are sometimes objects or symbols of worship by the occult practices forbidden by God. We all can be influenced by Satan and his demons.

Efforts to communicate with the dead or necromancy, magic, witchcraft and astrology are forbidden.

Deuteronomy 18: (NKJV), 10-12; There shall not be found among you anyone who makes his son or his daughter pass through the fire, or one who practices witchcraft, or sooth-sayer, or one who interprets omens, or a sor-cerer. Verse 11—or one who conjures spells, or a medium, or a spiritist, or one who calls up the dead. Verse 12—For all who do these things are an abomination to the Lord, and because of these abominations the Lord your God drives them out from before you.

If "pass through the fire" is a concept of test this is an abomination unto God. "Divination, (qesem), was a tactic the witches would use to predict an outcome known only to God. The pathways to information are known by Satan also. An example would be to read tea leafs or clouds to predict an outcome. The voodoo religion is very real, casting spells and even death. Witch denotes a form of magic. The root means "to cut up" and thus may refer to one who cuts up herbs and brews them for magical purposes. Wizard (yide oni), is a term related to the verb "to know" or to consult a familiar spirit. Necromancer: The Hebrew for this term means "one who asks of the dead".

We need to protect ourselves, our family, our love ones, and our church. The Bible in Ephesians 6, (NKJV), Verses 13-18 gives God's plan of protection.

Verse 13: Therefore take up the whole armor of God that you may be able to withstand in the evil day, and having done all, to stand.

Verse 14: Stand therefore, having girded your waist with truth, having put on the breastplate of "righteousness,"

Verse 15: and having shod your feet with the preparation of the gospel of peace;

Verse16: above all, taking the shield of faith with which you will be able to quench all the fiery darts of the wicked one.

Verse17: And take the helmet of "salvation, and the sword of the Spirit, which is the word of God";

Verse 18: praying always with all prayer and supplication in the Spirit, being watchful to this end with all perseverance and supplication for all the saints—

The whole armor of God consists of six pieces:

1. Truth is knowledge of the truth of God's Word. The ancient soldier's loins were girt about with a leather belt which held most of the other pieces of his armor in place. Similarly, the other pieces of the Christian's armor depend on and are held in place by his spiritual "belt" or his knowledge of the truth of scripture.

2. The breastplate of righteousness may be read the breastplate which is righteousness. It represents a holy character and moral conduct. Obedience to the truth; known produces a godly life of righteousness.

3. Preparation of the gospel of peace means eagerness that comes from the gospel of peace. That is as the Roman soldier wore special shoes called "caligae" on his feet, enabling him to advance against his enemy so the Christian must have on his feet (possess) a sense of "eagerness" to contend with Satan comes from the gospel of peace. The gospel gives peace to the believer, freeing him from anxiety though he advances against such a powerful opponent.

4. The shield of faith means taking God at His word by believing His promises. Such trust will protect one from doubts induced by Satan.

5. The helmet of salvation is the hope of salvation that is the certainty of assurance of salvation.

6. The sword of the Spirit, which is the Word of God. The Greek term rendered "word" is not logos, referring to the whole Word of God, but rhema, referring to certain portions or selected verses of scripture. Praying is required and means "stand" or is linked to this term. Without prayer God's armor is inadequate to achieve victory. Prayer is indispensable.....

119

BIBICAL DREAMS

We await the conformation from God as biblical dreams appear. Often they will be in symbols, vision like places, animals, objects, and they are usually quite difficult to interpret. God speaks to us in visions also as we begin to prophesize. This is only one of the spiritual gifts mentioned in the Bible.

On or about the last of December, 2009 I was to bring the Word at the Morgan County Correctional Complex, the ole Brushy Mtn. Prison in Morgan County, Tn. I began to ponder what the Lord would have me say. I was not too concerned God hadn't given me a word yet as time was getting closer to Sunday. I have learned to trust not in myself but to wait on the Lord. A person can only do so much without the unction of the Holy Ghost. So on Saturday the day before I was to speak. I continued to study to show myself approved and attempted to get a sermon ready, but still no Word from the Lord.

Then it happened, the night before I had a Biblical dream. I was standing in a prayer line looking behind me to the rear. There was nothing in the line but men. They were of different religions. A Catholic Father was in uniform. There were Muslim there. I was busy being friendly shaking hands and talking, when suddenly it was my turn and as I turned to face the front of the line there was no one there and I was confused.

So I fell to my knees and began to cry out (literally weep) to the Lord. As I prayed I noticed an Angel dressed in all White to my left. I knew the Holy presence was there but continued to cry out to the Lord and suddenly the Angel was in front of me and reached down and laid His hand of my head. Then the phone rang and of course interrupted or ended the dream. I didn't understand what it meant but when I began to preach at the prison I started by telling of the dream and asked if there was one there who could interrupt it for me.

I hadn't much more than mentioned the challenge when a brother stood up and said, he could tell me the meaning. So I listened.

He said that the line of all men indicated the prison. That the Angel reached down and touched me meant that I was now anointed and blessed to teach at the prison. I felt a sudden peace that He was right. Of course I didn't use my sermon notes.

We had an awesome service with almost half of the congregation of 100 or so came forward. There were some speaking in tongues and two claimed healing. I anointed some with oil and prayed for them—I know God was there and had answers for many. The next Sunday we had standing room only.

All glory is to God the Father as I seek His direction in this ministry. God is good!

I have had other Biblical dreams and always write them down as their meaning may not be obvious. Some of these were visionary in scope but one was definitely a warning. I'll close on dreams for now as they are for the interpreters who have this special calling. Write them down as soon as you awake remembering all the details as time will cause you to forget.

BATTLES AND STORMS ATTARCT GOD

Often it is here God will fulfill His promises and complete His plans. It is here you will find God at work in your life. He will not leave you or forsake you. It might be one of these seasons you will have to thaw your frozen faith and believe again. The portals of Heaven will open to those that believe and search their hearts for a renewal of mind and Spirit. Once you enter into Gods Will the going might not be easy but the rewards keep you doing what God has directed. Let God in if you are going through trials in your life. Trust that the storm will pass and realize we must pray the storm is only around us and not upon us.

Like Peter we too can walk on water if we will but get out of the boat of sin and step firmly upon the trust of Yahweh. If you have lost your job, or home, or car, we are reminded these are possessions here on earth and we must look forward to our eternal home. It is here our worry should become praise. So let us thank God for the storms around us. It is here our faith must not be frozen but reflect the temperature of blood, that blood of Jesus Christ shed on Calvary. I must remind you not to worry but pray yourself through the storm. The only perfect storm is one which is controlled by God Himself. He can quite the winds, calm the waters and bring peace back into your life.

Do not worry but Pray. A short time with God is better than a life time without Him. Ask Jesus back into your life. Let Him resolve these problems. Don't spend time worrying about those things you can't do anything about. He is here for you right now. If you bend your knee in prayer then the heart will assume the same position. Show us Oh Lord, the portal of your Kingdom in Christ. Let us not only seek the face of Yahweh but to come unto His Holy presence. God exists and is present with His people. Help us Lord to bring praise and communicate our love for you. As we kneel before thee allow the Holy Spirit to take control of our time left here on earth.

When the Glory comes there will be all manner of healings. There will be financial breakthroughs. Lives will commit to a calling from the Lord. Anytime you are present in this Glorious surrounding of God don't be afraid to step out for those answers. Let the Blood of Jesus thaw your frozen faith. He died a horrible death on the cross and we owe Him our life in return.

The First Epistle of Peter 1: (NKJV), 13-21 "Living before God our Father" instructs us; Therefore gird up the loins of your mind, be sober, and rest your hope fully upon the grace that is to be brought to you at the revelation of Jesus Christ; as obedient children, not conforming yourselves to the former lusts, as in your ignorance; but as He who called you is holy, you also be holy in all your conduct, because it is written, "Be Holy, for I am Holy."

And if you call on the Father, who without partiality judges according to each one's work, conduct yourselves throughout the time of your stay here in fear; knowing that you were not redeemed with corruptible things, like silver or gold, from your aimless conduct received by tradition from your fathers.

But with the precious blood of Christ, as of a lamb without blemish and without spot. He indeed was foreordained before the foundation of the world, but was manifest in these last times for you, who through Him believe in God, who raised Him from the dead and gave Him glory, so that your faith and hope are in God.

SO THAT FAITH AND HOPE ARE IN GOD, A-MAN

To receive the Holy Ghost for me took more courage to step out in the isle than it did to jump from a plane two miles in the sky. My first jump was at the young age of 60.

I thought Lord what if it doesn't happen then what? Is my faith in doubt for I know it is real. I have felt the power of God and do not question His power. The preacher said it was his last night and boy was I relieved for I knew it was too late to get a mess of the Holy

Ghost. So I said to myself if he only was there one more night I would step out in faith and walk the isle to receive this opportunity to be "slain in the Spirit".

Then he said, (the preacher)" he would stay another night" and I almost had a heart-attack. It is now Monday night and the church (New Covenant Life) in Lake City, Tn. was full. Joe was in the Spirit even more that night and he brought the sermon and then the alter call for those that wanted to experience this power and peace.

I was in the back of the church and that walk to the alter took an hour. There he was. Waiting for me as I came toward him I raised my hands in surrender. When he reached out to touch me it was as though someone hit me under the chin and I began to float backwards to where I can't remember.

I managed to crawl to the first pew and raise my weakened body to a sitting position. A lady there was laughing hysterically and she commented, "You should have seen yourself, it looked like something out of a Wild West movie". Trust in the Lord in all that you do. This is a solemn Godly occasion not to be taken lightly.

Thank God my faith was not frozen. He was with me all the way to the ground and all the way to the floor. I am His child and we are His disciples. Don't go through life with any doubt that God is real. His Holy Word will lead you on this journey. Holy Ghost have your way in our life and in this book.

In Mark 11: (NKJV) 22-24; Jesus said, "Have faith in God, For assuredly, I say to you, whoever says to this mountain, be removed and be cast into the sea, and does not doubt in his heart, but believes that those things he says will be done, he will have whatever he says, Therefore I say to you, whatever things you ask when you pray, believe that you receive them, and you will have them.

Here Jesus is telling us to have Faith, not Frozen Faith, that this faith when alive at 98.6 degrees is alive and is functional. Faith is a commitment of the mind and heart, manifest through our acceptance of the Messiah, controlled by His Holy Spirit.

I ask you not to condemn what you read in this book until you first are willing to step out in Un-Frozen Faith to experience the power of God. I know this is not for the weak at heart, or the religious folks but it is real just the same. Remember we serve a God who is Spirit and we must serve Him in the Spirit. You will have courage that was not available before Christ came into your life. The Apostles possessed a different kind of courage in order to be martyred. The Supernatural is just around the corner for those that have the boldness to step out.

Therefore if it is sin that is standing in the way of your next promotion or your prayer life is lacking or your un-belief has taken over I urge you to get right with God. The best way to change a bad habit is to replace it with a good one. If dark secrets have come between you and Christ and you know longer feel His closeness, don't wait until it is too late.

It is never God that goes away, but the influence of the flesh which clouds our vision. Thus we are taken out of His Will. He will not let you rest in peace until His child becomes obedient. Be still and know when God is trying to get your attention. He is an Omni God that offers Himself to live in us through the Holy Spirit. As we are weak in this human body God will be our strength if we will rely on Him.

The flesh is made stronger when we stray from the Word. We know perfection is not possible given our humanist nature and only one was perfect and He is the Christ. But greater is He who is in me than he who is in the world. Lord let our example fill the voids of the past and enrich our soul with the spiritual gifts. Let not the evil man control our life and when we are out of touch surround us with your protective hedge. Lord I speak blessings upon the readers of this book.

Yes, we are born with an appetite but only God can satisfy our true hunger. The appetite of the flesh will only add to the flesh where the appetite of the soul will bring into focus

God Almighty. In John 6: 35 (NKJV); Jesus said, "I am the bread of life. He who comes to Me shall never hunger, and he who believes in Me shall never thirst."

Are you drowning in Sin? Jesus can lift you up and dry those tears of sorrow. Is Sin in your life taking you to the pits of Hell? It is time regardless of age to step up to higher ground. Put distance between where you are and where you expect to be.

Proverbs 3: (NKJV) 5-6; says to trust in the Lord with all your heart. And lean not on your own understanding; in all your ways acknowledge Him. And He shall direct your paths.

As you live your lives do you find it harder and harder to maintain focus on what God has in store for you? Has darkness over taken the Light? Jesus is the truth and the Light.

1st John 1: (NKJV) 7; Tells us but if we walk in the light as He is in the light, we have fellowship with one another, and the Blood of Jesus Christ His Son cleanses us from all sin.

WHEN THE BATTLES AND STORMS COME UN-FREEZE YOUR FROZEN FAITH

That tiny light at the end of the tunnel can become the center point of your life if you will but let God in and take control. It will magnify within you and His brilliance will shine that no jewel can match and cannot be contained. Many of our battles are nothing more than spiritual warfare manifest in us through our imagination. These thoughts become the focal point that will control our choice between good and evil. The devil will use our past to cause division within us. That is why we don't take our baggage with us after we repent. If God forgives us why should we even remember it? If Satan can manipulate your thoughts and convince you that you have failed or what is the use anyway you will keep doing the same things (sin) over and over. He has won the battle. But if you will not quit but continue to repent and ask God to help fight this battle, the battle is yours, thanks to God.

The way we do this is through praise and worship for the satanic forces cannot dwell in God's presence. Thank God for the battle at hand and praise Him for He is Lord, you cannot fail. Ask Him to allow this test to become your testimony. You have just invoked spiritual warfare against the devil and God has never lost a battle or a war. If you have never done this I challenge you to try if faith that God will intervene on your behalf. What did Paul say," Less of me Lord and more of you". Give the spiritual person control over your life, your finances, your health, and your eternity. The Bible will teach you the way of life.

CHAPTER 5

THE FIRE OF FAITH IS
KINDLED BY PRAYER

Prayer is truly the heartbeat of the church. When I first began my prison ministry at the MCCX in Tn., I was assigned to Unit # 1 which is a portion of the prison that segregates the incarcerated from the population of the prison. It is here for whatever reason certain men are housed for their own protection. The reasons vary and I don't consider that important for a volunteer chaplain chosen to share Yahweh with those who will listen and take part. When the church call was given in unit # 1, I didn't know exactly where God wanted me to go with His message of the Gospel of Jesus Christ. So I explained my presence was not about me but about them and their salvation and so I did a show of hands to see what they expected from me. The very first class said we want to know how to pray to your

God so that we know He is there for us. Some explained they prayed but it seemed like their prayers only went to the ceiling. Hallelujah to the Lord. I felt like I hit pay dirt on the first scoop of dirt. We know "prayer" is the heartbeat of the church. We are the church for our bodies are the Holy Temple that Christ's Holy presence resides.

I was excited to embark on another mission. In fact each time I go into the prison I still get nervous much the same as when I go to Brazil, Peru, or any other far away country. The men here are hungry for the Word and many are saturated with the Holy Spirit. (Some even as "Saul" that become "Paul", the apostle of our Lord that wrote over 25% of the New Testament.) These men understand because of wrong choices or decisions in their life what it is to lose their freedom. The only difference in them and a lot of us on the outside is they got caught and we didn't. Does it matter either way since Sin is Sin and God knows everything in life?

THE FIRE OF FAITH IS KINDLED BY PRAYER

Sometimes I get wrapped up in the Lord and it is easier to just let the Holy Spirit have His way in my life and this is why I sometimes speak in my childhood language most don't understand but God does. It is the utterance before God. This is why I weep when I am happy and cannot seem to tell God in words how much I love Him.

The prison church began with a Holy Ghost prayer, not from my humanist spirit but from the one that took up residency in my body. We always passed a prayer request so the guys could write down the desires of their heart. Some through many years of lock-up had built up the wall between emotions and reality. I think I might have been the first man in many years they saw weep un-ashamed before man and God. It is okay for a man to cry, and this is to you macho minded men. The prayer list became so important that they would ask me for one if I was slow in passing it around. In fact we began to hear praise reports after praise report that I to begin to add my desires to the list. They began to see their prayers being answered as I encouraged each one to seek intimate communal prayer with the Lord. Often after leaving the prison I would continue to pray over the prayer list. Their names were left off but we serve an Omni God that does not need an introduction of who we are.

As we began to study the Word and how to pray I was amazed at the spirituality and the zeal they began to develop. Their boldness became apparent as some would want to close the service in prayer. Before, they were reserved and a bit backward to do much of anything but through the power of the Holy Spirit they displayed the Christian attitude you would expect.

In general we would open up with prayer only capable when the Holy Spirit was present:

WE SHARE OUR HEART WITH YOU OH LORD! AND ASK YOU TO SHARE YOUR HEART WITH US THROUGH YOUR HOLY WORD.

FORGIVE US OUR SINS AND SHORT COMINGS.

ALLOW OUR CONSTANT WAITING TO DEVELOP OUR PATIENCE IN THEE.

LORD MIX OUR FAITH AND PATIENCE TO OVERCOME THIS ADVERSITY.

ALLOW THIS FELLOWSHIP AND STUDY OF YOUR WORD TO BRING FORTH THE FRUIT OF THE SPIRIT.

HELP US TO REALIZE AND INCREASE THE HOLY SPIRIT'S PRESENCE IN US.

WE THANK YOU FOR THIS SUPERNATURAL POWER TO LIVE OUR LIFE AND BECOME MORE LIKE YAHSHUA.

PROTECT AND BLESS OUR FAMILY AND LOVE ONES.

WE CLAIM YOUR HEDGE FOR THEIR PROTECTION; PLACE ANGELS IN THEIR LIFE WHILE WE ARE GONE.

Often we would pray one for another. Lift each other up as trials and tribulations are present even in this life. To pray is to manifest our Faith in God. Prayer is the most powerful tool we have as Christians. The guys became more and more convinced as they learned to pray. Hearing each other proclaim that their prayers were being answered got us all excited.

We began with the nine categories of prayers:
1. The prayer of Confession is necessary before we can have communion with God. We know that even David cried out to God for repentance.
2. The prayer of Thanksgiving is simply thanking God for what He has done in our life.
3. A prayer of Petition is making a personal request of God.
4. The prayer of Intercession is making a request of God on behalf of another.

5. The prayer of Praise adoring God for who He is will certainly usher in His Holy presence.

6. The prayer of Commitment exercises our boldness and willingness to be used by God and express's our loyalty personally to God.

7. The prayer of Forgiveness is seeking mercy for personal sin or the sin of others.

8. Never forget the prayer of Benediction as this is to request for God's blessings for us as well as others in our life.

9. We have the prayer of Confidence which affirms God's all-sufficiency and the believers security in His love.

WE SHOULD ALWAYS ASK GOD TO BLESS OUR FOOD

We have said that Prayer is the Heartbeat of the Church and it is the avenue we should use through Christ into the very Throne Room of God. The Holy Ghost power of praying will bring results. If your prayers feel like they are going no further than the ceilings then you need to examine yourself, there is probably the hindrance of Sin in your life.

You can never accomplish your mission or goal as a Christian without prayer. You can never take your seat of authority God has in store for you without prayer. We are destined to enter into the path God has chosen for us. Each of us as a vessel of God must be willing to be used is prayed-up and in place in the center of His Will.

When you step over into the arena God has called you to, the anointing will be present. As you begin to identify your place in life or the seat of authority then occupy those areas where God has granted you dominion. God will bless you. Align your life according to the Word of the Bible and in all ways acknowledge Him and He shall direct your path.

We know the FIRE OF FAITH, is kindled by our prayers. Never be embarrassed by only a few words to God. He knows our heart and quite often the man that prays much has said less. We not only need God's forgiveness but we must not have un-forgiveness against our brother. His forgiveness is necessary also. Ask God to forgive us daily and repent of all un-acknowledged sin as well.

Never hurry your prayer life as you ponder your thoughts. As you pray, listen to what God has to say in return. Remember God's time is not our time therefore we must wait for the spiritual realm to move. Remember God is Spirit; allow intimacy to develop as your faith grows. There is no conversation with God without prayer. You can see by this how important it is to pray. Be still and know He is God.

Remember there are many Hindrances to Prayer:

1. Sin; Your iniquities can and will separate you from God. Only sincere repentance can repair this hindrance.
2. Un-Forgiveness; if we who are imperfect and prone to mistakes want mercy and acceptance before a perfect and Holy God, we must be more gracious toward those whose flaws affect us. We must forgive, if we want forgiveness.
3. Idolatry; if there is anything that occupies the place in the heart designed for God, then this is an idol. This can be a spiritual matter as mentioned in Ezekiel 14;—Idolatry will be punished.
4. Unbelief; you must believe, ask in faith, with no doubting.
5. Selfishness; Prayer must be appropriate not for a wrong motive. Don't let SELF be at the center as praying amiss mentioned in James 4: 3.

Remember when you go beyond words you will come to the sweetest level of prayer. In prayer it is better to have heart without words, than words without heart. Unity with God is the heart of prayer. This is why we must listen for His voice. This is the Oneness we all search for in Christ. We must be liberated from the flesh and transformed to walk in the

Spirit. Prayer is a precious gift of communication that goes beyond understanding.

Once again: If you will but "open your Bible", repent of your daily sins, your un-acknowledge sin hidden because your conscience no longer recognizes it as sin, inequities and even abominations against God and praise Him for who He is. Combine your human voice with the Holy Word of God and be grafted into the realm of the supernatural of the Holy Spirit using Biblical language then God will hear the voice of the redeemed.

You must yield to God's action. Let Him come near. Let Him surround you with His agape love. Listen to His voice and know He is God. He will speak to you sometimes in that still small voice or through His Word, or through dreams, and through visions. Seek His Face and His presence will come.

It's okay to weep deeply over the grace of God and Its embrace. Tears have a way of cleansing the soul. It is through God's grace we are saved. As a child of God we are heirs to His Kingdom.

Let the Bible give you language to pray or express the depth of you encounters using the word substitution method. Simply place the name you are praying for in place of the name used in the Bible.

An example of this might be: In John 3: (NKJV) 16 Jesus is saying For God so loved the world that He gave His only begotten

Son, that whoever believes in Him should not perish but have everlasting life.

If you are leading someone to Christ you might say, "George", or "Karla", God so loved the world that He gave, etc...

The same system could be used in a healing prayer or any of those mentioned earlier. When you are reading your Bible practice this for someone God lays on your heart.

He is watching over you. Allow peace and joy to come into your life. Prayer should be the key of the day and the lock at night. When the door-way or portal to Heaven is not open we must find the blockage. If it is Sin, then repent and renew you mind.

Sin is not only a mistake but it can become deadly or a fatal mistake. It is a toxin to the soul. Prayer will make a man cease from sin, or sin will entice a man to cease from prayer. Prayer is a shield to the soul, a sacrifice to God, and scourge for Satan. Prayer is the defining factor in the war with the Flesh. The spirit is willing, but the flesh is usually found weak.

The presence or absence of prayer is often the simple difference between defeat and victory.

The battleground of Sin is in your mind.

THE RIGHT INSTRUCTION, FROM YAHWEH, THE GOD OF ISREAL

Your Mind is not a playground and every thought that drifts by is a fact of life and is what makes us different than an animal such as a dog. A dog can learn facts but is not designed to think or reason. It can be trained and molded to do our will such as Satan will do to us. We as humans possess the ability to think or reason and to make choices between good or evil. It is here we have the option to not only receive a thought but we now have the choice to retain this thought and build upon it or remove it from our storage the mind. If it is stored it is now planted in our heart, the door way to our soul. Then the flesh (body) becomes vulnerable to wrong choices.

Philippians 4: (NKJV) 4-9 are great instructions; Verse 4. Rejoice in the Lord always. Again I will say, rejoice! Verse 5. Let your gentleness be known to all men. The Lord is at hand. Verse 6. Be anxious for nothing but in everything by prayer and supplication, with thanksgiving, let your requests be make known to God; Verse 7. And the peace of God, which surpasses all understanding, will guard your hearts and minds through Christ Jesus. Verse 8. Finally, brethren, whatever things are true, whatever things are noble, whatever things are just, whatever are lovely, whatever things are of good report, if there is any virtue and if there is anything praiseworthy—meditate on these things. Verse 9. The things which you learned and received and heard and saw in me, these do, and the God of peace will be with you.

If you have thoughts contrary to this instruction cast it out immediately. Do not let this thought become the seed that becomes the worm, mentioned in Mark 9: (NKJV) 44-48. This worm can and will send you one step closer to Hell. It can and will close down your conscience. You will see no wrong in your actions. You will be in harm's way and could possible interrupt your walk with God.

Verse 44. Jesus says, where, Their worm does not die, and the fire is not quenched.

Verse 45. And if your foot causes you to sin, cut it off. It is better for you to enter life lame, rather than having two feet, to be cast into hell, into the fire that shall never be quenched—

Verse 46. Where, There worm does not die and the fire is not quenched.

Verse 47. And if your eye causes you to sin, pluck it out. It is better for you to enter the kingdom of God with one eye, rather than having two eyes, to cast into hell fire—

Verse 48. Where Their worm does not die, And the fire is not quenched

Verse 49. For everyone will be seasoned with fire and every sacrifice will be seasoned with salt.

If you have allowed the Sin of the "worm", your repeated wrong choice to be planted in your soul and your conscience fails to detect it as Sin because of the many repetitions the body performs this act it is obvious that Satan has a strong hold in your life. It is important for Jesus to mention it three times.

I urge you to repent of any and all unacknowledged Sin.

2nd Corinthians 10: (NKJV) 3; For though we walk in the flesh, we do not war according to the flesh.

Verse 4. For the weapons of our warfare are not carnal but mighty in God for pulling down strongholds.

Verse 5. Casting down arguments and every high thing that exalts itself against the knowledge of God, bringing every thought into captivity to the obedience of Christ.

For more knowledge of protection go to Ephesians 6: 10-18 and review the "Whole Armor of God".

Paul tells us in Romans 12: Do not be conformed to this world, but be transformed by the RENEWING of your mind, that you may prove what is that good and acceptable will of God.

When you call time out and enter into your prayer closet simply begin by repenting of your sins. If you have any un-acknowledged sin put it on the platter also, and review the beginning of the Lord's prayer. Thy Kingdom come on earth as it is in Heaven and approach the Throne Room with the desires of your heart and know, with faith, that Gods hears your every cry. Often these request or prayers will be answered in God's time. So understand the miracle may be instant or truly in God's Time, as He knows the big picture. Our time here on earth is nothing more than a test to see how you live your life. Time is the master of life but God is the final say so. Allow your time in prayer to be the testimony of your earthly belief that you will live for Him. Lord knowing that words are not enough to show our gratitude but that we might live for thee in a salt covenant is our prayer. Our walk shall bring forth the works of the spirit. Show me a lamp unto my feet and a light unto my path that my journey might bring glory and praise to your Holy name.

THE LORDS PRAYER

In Matthew 6: (NKJV) 5-13; Jesus tells us about the model prayer given to the Apostles.

Verse 5; "And when you pray, you shall not be like the hypocrites. For they love to pray standing in the synagogues and on the cor- ners of the streets, that they may be seen by men. Assuredly, I say to you, they have their reward.

Verse 6; "But you, when you pray, go into your room, and when you have shut your door, pray to your Father who is in the secret place; and you Father who sees in secret will reward you openly.

Verse 7; "And when you pray, do not use vain repetitions as the heathen do For they think that they will be heard for their many words.

Verse 8; "Therefore do not be like them. For your Father knows the things you have need of before you ask Him.

Verse 9; In this manner, therefore, pray:

Our Father in heaven, Hallowed be Your name.

(Comment ;) This is commonly known as the Lord's Prayer. This is the very prayer Jesus taught His disciples. "Our Father" denotes the paternal need for us His children. "Hallowed" be Your name sets apart from normal respect to a Sacred tone. This gives God His due respect.

Verse 10; Your kingdom come Your will be done.

(Comment ;) Declare that His kingdom priorities shall be established even before you enter heaven. With this thought in mind use the Kingdom here on earth and realize His Holy Power is here for those that truly believe, taking advantage of the Kingdom Power.

Verse 11; Give us this day our daily bread.

(Comments ;) Be thankful for you daily bread and ask God to bless it to be the purified nourishment for the body.

Verse 12; And forgive us our debts, As we forgive our debtors,

(Comment ;) We need God's forgiveness and we need to forgive others. Love God and Love our neighbors as our self.

Verse 13; And do not lead us into temptation, But deliver us from the evil one. For Yours is

the kingdom and the power and the glory forever. Amen

(Comment ;) Here we are asking God to deliver
us from Satan. Jesus goes on to tell us if we
forgive men there trespasses, your heavenly
Father will also forgive you. But if you do not
forgive men their trespasses, neither will your
Father forgive your trespasses.

"KICKING THE ADDICTIONS"

If you think you might have a problem with Addictions, you most likely do. America is a nation of people addictive to the very good life here in this country. It is this spoiled condition of our very nature that lends itself to addictions. You might think I have a few bad habits but I wouldn't say they were a dependency, certainly not an addiction.

Yes, I drink coffee every morning, several cups a day and have for a long time. If coffee is not available I settle for a soft drink or two. I like to listen to music or c/d's on the way to and from work or school. Music is a big part of my life. Yes, I listen to all kinds of music and some is junk. When I get to the work or school arena I need to get the latest gossip of the day. You know what I mean. Of course you need to tell your closest friend. This news is too good to keep quite. I trust my friend not to tell even though I promised to keep it secret. If a typical morning or day is lived this way, day in and out begins and ends this way, you have addictions. I am an addict. There, now I've said it.

We are a nation of addicts. We are spoiled and are accustomed to the easy life in America. This easy life is that we take for granted, because of abundance our human nature indulges in what the flesh desires. This is also true for the secular society; Hollywood the influenced country we live in. Sex, drugs, alcohol, and pornography are rampant in this now generation. We are becoming a Godless nation forgetting the Cross and Great Commission. If this is you I urge you to come out of denial long enough to look at your life.

Now back to the typical day. If you started by having coffee or soft drinks and indicated it might take more than a couple to get through the day, has this become a habit? On the way to work or school did you listen to a varied of music. Was any of it Christian music? After you reached your destination, was gossip the first order of the day?

Webster's dictionary suggests an addict is to devote or give (one self) habitually or compulsively. When you do something over and over it becomes a habit, then you can become addictive to this habit which starts with doing it the first time. We could go on and on with modern day interpretations that would better suit our own experiences dealing with what a habit is or when it becomes an addiction. This concept will place us into denial. When we begin to live in denial of what we do and are afraid we have lost control of our habits we begin to lie to our self.

The worst lies are the ones we tell ourselves. Once you reach the addiction stage moderation is impossible. We must stop the activity or substance and deal with it. I would advise you to pray what is said in John 15: (NKJV) verse 7; If you abide in Me, and My words abide in you, you will ask what you desire, and it shall be done for you. Also mentioned in Hebrews 12: (NKJV) 1; Therefore we also, since we are surrounded by so great a cloud of witnesses, let us lay aside every weight, and the sin which so easily ensnares us, and let us run with endurance the race that is set before us, and Verse 2; looking unto Jesus, the author and finisher of our faith, who for the joy that was set before Him endured the cross, despising the shame, and has sat down at the right hand of the throne of God. The heroes of faith and their witness of faith provided by their living example proclaim to lay aside all living weights. In other words don't let addictions or sin of the flesh weight you down so that you might be strong in the race of life living for the cross of Calvary.

I have done a complete fast on occasions some for 21 days at a time. This is not to lift me up but to give God all the glory, but I had issues in my life that required fasting. If you want to seek the face of Yahshua then fast. You would think I would miss food as hunger crept in but to my surprise the headache came from my lack of coffee that grown to dependency at several cups a day.

If habits in your life become passions or compulsion you suffer addictions. It may only be soft core in nature at this time but is it sin lurking in your life? The process of denial is a form of deception which keeps us from healing. We can fool ourselves and others but God knows our inner most secrets.

The Bible says this about gossip. In Proverbs 11 ;(NKJV) 13; A talebearer reveals secrets, But he who is of a faithful spirit conceals a matter. Choose your friends wisely. Gossip no matter how insignificant will develop an unfaithful spirit. When a promise is made it should be honored.

Denial is a relief when we don't want the truth. Excuses, alibis and rationalizations are the products as well as the crutches used when we won't face when our habits have become not just passion but sin.

We all suffer a bit of brain damage either through denial or excessively use which becomes a dependency. The hard drugs will take there tolls and softer ones will lead to a stronger ones. These addictions have been linked to certain chemicals released in the brain. Even that simple act of drinking too much coffee or soda starts by choice. We have started with soft core addictions but more serious ones surface latter as hard core.

Illicit drugs taken sometimes because of peer pressure, by choice, or for recreational purposes can certainly lead to dependency. Repeated use of marijuana, cocaine, or crack causes a surge in levels of a brain chemical we will just call the feel good sensation. Once our brain experiences this, it will call for more and more until the feel good dependency level is obtained. Alcohol is the legal drug of choice for many. This drug has wrecked countless lives and killed many. Many narcotics from pharmaceutical companies are acquired and taken illegal.

These drugs of passion or compulsive behavior are early stages of addiction, corruption and Sin. When Sin takes over a soul the body is not far behind. Our self-esteem suffers and our walk with God is not only affected but is usually ended. You will become complacent with each act allowing your feel good substance to take control. Addiction is the psychic enemy of mankind. If you are interested in taking steps to stop, I like what is said in Ephesians 2: (NKJV) 8; For by grace you have been saved through faith, and that not of yourselves, it is the gift of God.

This is the same God given Grace that gave us salvation. It is free and is abundant for those that will only ask, believing they have received. Not only is Grace undeserved kindness by which our salvation is given, but it is also the power-word describing the Holy Spirit's operational means. Grace is a force as well as a Favor, a verb as well as a noun.

Don't let these attachments make in-roads into your soul. This subtle unction will cripple your walk with God. Your spiritual experience is part of our quest to find God. We were made to communicate and fellowship with God not only through prayer and reading the Bible but knowing God is there for us.

Sin is magnified and increased by addictions. What starts out to be a onetime simple act can and will come between you and our Lord. The habits of our everyday life when merged with daily addictions will suffer your prayer life. It will put space between you and God. I urge you to graft your spiritual walk with those chores and choices of life in your daily living to reflect praise and glory to the Father. Sin is what turns us away from Gods Love. It turns us away from love for ourselves, and away from love for one another.

We are reminded by Jesus in the gospel of Mark 12: (NKJV) 29-31; (Here Jesus answered the Scribes) Jesus answered him, "The first of all the commandments is, Hear, O Israel, the Lord our God, the Lord is one.

Verse 30: And you shall love the Lord your God with all your heart, with all your soul, with all your mind, and with all your strength. This is the first commandment.

Verse 31: And the second, like it, is this: You shall love your neighbor as yourself. There is no other commandment greater than these.

If you frequently repress your desire to love, could it be a result of fear? I trusted that person and now look at all the hurt and shame in my life. Never again will I let my guard down. Have you ever had these thoughts? Often it will take time before you can love or trust again. It is a normal human response to repress our feelings. When we repress our desire for love the emotions migrate to the back burner. This may be when we begin to par-take of drugs or alcohol. This might be that time we try illicit drugs or could it be to get even with that person. Often wrong sex, or lust gone wild will lead to more sex. But he said we will get married and now I am pregnant. Now what!

This is the norm and not the exception. Once again we open ourselves up to sin. The devil cast his net of doubt upon those unsuspecting individuals who choose to go against the grain of a Holy and Pure life. Once again I remind you that the sin lurking in your life will force you into denial, repression, depression and addiction.

If you have a sensing in the spirit that God has drifted from you, could it be that innocent habits have become addictions? Could it be those addictions have become the sin in your life. I can tell you, "yes" sin will separate us from God. God has not drifted from us but sin in our life has separated us and God. No longer can we walk and talk freely to the Lord.

No longer is our prayer life in phase with His will. No longer is our faith present there for us in life's emergencies. No longer is our walk representative of that as a follower of Christ. Your seeds of destined handed down to later generations is altered by your decision to rid addictions from your life. Don't disrupt Gods plan for you and your family to the third and fourth generation because of these Sins.

You cannot change the past no more than you can the future without the Holy presence of Christ in your life. The present state of life is the only one we need to participate. It is here we must surround ourselves with the Agape Love of God, which is more than abundant. The darkness of addiction hides the true size of Fear and Lies which engulfs our very soul. This darkness becomes habitual in nature as we seek the shadows of Sin. Only one trace of light from the Lord will reveal the presence of the darkness of Satan. John 3: (NKJV) 19; And this is the condemnation, that light is come into the world, and men loved darkness rather than light, because their deeds were evil.

If power is your addiction (control freak) and you will do anything to feed this demonic spirit, does it really matter if someone is different than you thought after the courtship. Why begin the process of trying to change them? The important thing is a mutual relationship and not my way or the highway.

Don't be taken captive by this controlling attitude. Don't succumb to those miserable quirks which have gone berserk. Guard verbal abuse from taking its toll with the people you love most. Don't let Satan destroy your relationship.

PUT YOUR FAITH IN GOD

It is not your intelligence, your abilities, your friends, yourself or your bank account that will give you real confidence. Put your trust in Jesus. Accept the Trinity; God the Father, God the Son, and God the Holy Ghost. Trust in Him completely and stay rooted in the Word, Pray only in the Holy Ghost and seek the Kingdom. Seek ye First the Kingdom of God and all things will be handed unto you.

You could lose your bank account overnight. You can become disabled through sickness or an accident and suddenly lose your ability even to walk. Your intelligence is a gift of God and Satan can manipulate your very sanity. He can cause you to desire those things which will affect your judgment. Wrong desires will rule our life and damage priorities in life.

Proverbs 16: (NKJV) 9 says, A man's heart plans his ways, But the Lord directs his steps.

Therefore keep your heart tuned to the unction of the Holy Spirit. Learn to feel the gentile tug at what is right and what is wrong. Proceed with God in all that you do and carry your part of the cross. His load is light and your rewards in Heaven are great.

Psalms 5: (NKJV) 12 conforms this. For You, O Lord, will bless the righteous; with favor You will surround him as with a shield. His shield is the protection against the fiery darts of Satan. As followers of Christ the devil is our enemy. He came to steal, kill, and send us to Hell. Satan the opponent to God is a fallen angel. He tries to take away people's happiness by blocking God's purposes in our life. He manipulates us through temptations and deception. He is also called Beelzebub, the evil one, and Lucifer. The devil has superhuman power but can be resisted with God's help. His powers are limited to what God permits. Satan is served by other fallen angels known as Demons. Christians cannot be possessed by demons but they can be influenced. We cannot serve two masters.

We as Followers of Christ must take on the character of Him. Even with our best intentions and willpower is not enough. Only the Holy Spirit has the power to do what is necessary to convict us of sin and draw us to repentance so that we might be redeemed. Christ paid the sin debt on Calvary that we might be forgiven and it is through His shed blood, death and resurrection on the third day that completes our salvation.

Learn to know God's voice. Philippians 2: (NKJV) says, for it is God who works in you both to will and to do for His good pleasure. Mention the "power of the Holy Spirit," and many people think of miraculous demonstrations and intense emotions. But most of the time the Holy Spirit's power is released in a quite unassuming way that you aren't even aware of. He often nudges us with that 'gentile whisper".

We are reminded of Elijah at the mountain of Horeb, which is the mountain of God. The Bible tells us in 1st Kings 19: (NKJV) 8-13; So he (Elijah) arose, and ate and drank; and he went in the strength of that food forty days and forty nights as far as Horeb, the mountain of God. And there he went into a cave, and spent the night in that place; and behold, the word of the Lord came to him, and He said to him, "What are you doing here, Elijah?" So he said, "I have been very zealous for the Lord God of hosts; for the children of Israel have forsaken Your covenant, torn down Your altars, and killed Your prophets with the sword. I alone am left; and they seek to take my life." Then He said, "go out, and stand on the mountain before the Lord," And behold, the Lord passed by, and a great and strong wind tore into the mountains and broke the rocks in pieces before the Lord, but the Lord was not in the wind; and after the wind an earthquake, but the Lord was not in the earthquake; and after the earthquake a fire, but the Lord was not in the fire; and after the fire a "still small voice". So it was, when Elijah heard it, that he wrapped his face in his mantle and went out and stood in the entrance of the cave. Suddenly a voice came to him, and said, "What are you doing here, Elijah?"

This illustrates when we seek God it is not always His response to answer us with earth shattering actions but often it is the "tiny voice from within". He will speak using different methods for different people. Once you have received a mid-course correction or a new direction, peace will enter your soul. It is sometimes not easy to hear His voice that is why we must depend on the Holy Spirit to speak to our natural spirit. Our connection with God is through the Holy Spirit. Stay connected and be still and know that He is God.

Often that urge is to cry or show emotions. Sometimes it is a feeling that makes us want to run or dance before the Lord. Nothing has changed with God since the days of King David. God is the same today, yesterday and tomorrow.

Learn to know when God is speaking to you but do not mistake it for intelligence of the natural spirit or flesh. If you walk in the Spirit, stay in the Word, pray constantly and seek the Face of God then there will be no mistake when God is trying to get your attention or speak to you. The "Secret" is Christ lives in us.

God's Spirit lives in each of us that is born again. It is up to us to separate flesh from spirit. It is up to us to separate the natural spirit from the Spirit we received when we accepted Christ as our personal savior. The boldness or strength can be obtained just by asking God. This new zeal in our heart will confirm Gods connection with our soul. Above all pray for wisdom with its ability to here and know the right choices or decisions for your life. In essence God is saying get on with your life and yes you will continue to make mistakes but God is a God of abundant grace and He will forgive those that "repent".

None of us are perfect. Jesus, the Messiah is the only one that lived a sinless life and He paid the price on the cross. God sent His only begotten Son that we might have life ever after. Repent daily and our sins will become less as we take on the character of Christ as His Spirit works in us. God is working in you, giving us the desire to obey Him and the power to do what pleases Him. Christ likeness is not produced by imitation, but by inhabitation, as we allow Christ to live through us.

God enjoys watching us use the talents and abilities He has given us. God intentionally gifted us differently for His enjoyment. He has made some to be athletic and some to be analytical. You may be gifted at mechanics or at music or a hundred other skills. All of these activities can bring a smile to God's Face.

161

You don't bring glory or pleasure to God by hiding your talents or abilities or by trying to be someone else. We have heard the parable of five talents where Jesus showed us that if we have a talent we must use this ability or we bring displeasure to Him. We are told to increase our abilities in order to bring glory to the Kingdom.

In Matthew 25: (NKJV) Jesus talks about the parable of the Talents. In Verse 24 and 25 He says, then he who had received the one talent came and said, "Lord I knew you to be a hard man, reaping where you have not sown, and gathering where you have not scattered seed. 25; And I was afraid, and went and hid your talent in the ground, Look, there you have what is yours."

Verses 26 through 29 deals with Jesus's answer: Jesus said, "But His Lord answered and said to him, you wicked and lazy servant, you knew that I reap where I have not sown, and gather where I have not scattered seed. So you ought to have deposited my money with the bankers, and at my coming I would have received back my own with interest. Therefore take the talent from him, and give it to him who has ten talents. For to everyone who has, more will be given, and he will have abundance; but from him who does not have, even what he has will be taken away.

We are encouraged to use our talents and abilities God gave us. We are instructed to be fruitful with these gifts and bring glory to God. Make pleasing God the goal of your life.

Bear in mind that we are nothing more than dust and without God we are nothing. When He breathed life into our dust and we become mankind we were made to bring praise and glory to His name. Don't hide or discard our God given talents. Trade your talents and multiply them. You are on a win-win course and cannot lose by using those talents God gave you. God also gains pleasure in watching you enjoy His creation. We are His "first fruits". Our body, soul and spirit is who we are. We are His creation and truly have been a disappointment most of our existence on earth. He doesn't expect us to be perfect since sin entered our life but He demands obedience. It is by this function we can remain in His favor. He is not a respecter of persons. Even the Jewish people which are the chosen ones and the apple of His eye have been punished many times for their disobedience. He will watch over as we grow spiritually just as we watch over our children as they mature. What God looks at is the attitude of the heart, which is the window of your soul.

God is looking for a few good people, the Noah's in this 21ˢᵗ century, people willing to live for the pleasure of God. The Bible says in Psalm14: (NKJV) 2; The Lord looks down from

Heaven upon the children of men, to see if there are any who understand, who seek God. Won't you become a God chaser?

In John 20: (NKJV) The later part of verse 19 Jesus said "peace be with you." Continuing on in verses 20 and 21, When He had said this, He showed them His hands and His side. Then the disciples were glad when they saw the Lord. So Jesus said to them again, "Peace to you! As the Father has sent Me, I also send you."

Verses' 22-23 finishes the Apostles Commission; And when He had said this, He breathed on them, and said to them, "RECEIVE THE HOLY SPIRIT." 23; If you forgive the sins of any, they are forgiven them; if you retain the sins of any, they are retained.

The Apostles went forth with the complete power of God. Forgiveness is a key part of the gospel of Jesus Christ. When we forgive, cancel, someone's sin against us, the light of God will shine through us into their darkened heart, enabling them to see God in us. We must forgive in order for God to forgive us. This instruction is as hard as praying for you enemies.

Mark 11; (NKJV) 24-25; reminds us to do this before we pray. Therefore I say to you, whatever things you ask when you pray, believe that you receive them, and you will have them. 25; and whenever you stand praying, If you have anything against anyone, forgive him, that your Father in Heaven may also forgive you your trespasses.

THOUGHTS TO PONDER

"Negative Thoughts"—declare "out loud", God perfects all things that concern me. Psalm 138: (NKJV) 8; The Lord will perfect that which concerns me; Your mercy, O Lord, endures forever; Do not forsake the works of Your hands.

"I Am In Charge"—Deuteronomy 28: (NKJV) 13; And the Lord will make you the head and not the tail; you shall be above only, and not be beneath, if you heed the commandments of the Lord your God, which I command you today, and are careful to observe them.

"Create Faith Energy"—Faith comes from by hearing, and hearing by the word of God mentioned in Romans 10: (NKJV) 17. Therefore you hear the Word every time you speak the Word. 2nd Corinthians 4: (NKJV) 13; and since we have the same spirit of faith, according to what is written, "I believed and therefore I spoke," we also believe and therefore speak.

"Fire Your Negative Attitudes"—Admit negative attitudes never produce good. When you stay aligned with these attitudes, you produce negative power. Jesus said in Matthew 18: (NKJV) 19 and 20; Again I say to you that if two of you agree on earth concerning anything that they ask, it will be done for them by My Father in Heaven. And verse 20 goes on to say, "For where two or three are gathered together in My name, I am there in the midst of them." Ask someone to pray with you.

"Agree With God"—Whether you feel it or not, see it or not, demand of yourself to speak words of victory from the scripture that God has supplied. Romans 8: (NKJV) 31 and 32; What then shall we say to these things? If God is for us, who can be against us? 32; He who did not spare His own Son, but delivered Him up for us all, how shall He not with Him also freely "give us all things? Verse 37; Yet in all these things we are more than conquerors through Him who loved us.

"Recognize God Has Something Better For You"—Hebrews 11: (NKJV) 40; God has something better for us. Expect it Look forward to it.

"God Will Provide"—Philippians 4: (NKJV) 19; And my God shall supply all your need according to His riches in glory by Christ Jesus.

"Take Charge of What Can Be With Your Words"—Job 22: (NKJV) 28; says, You shall decree a thing. And it shall be established to you, and it will be established for you; So light will shine on your ways.

THE BIBLE IS THE DIVINE WORD OF GOD

The Bible is not one book. It is a collection of 66 books written by 40 different authors. They came from a variety of backgrounds. Some were shepherds, fisherman, doctors, kings, prophets and others. The 66 books were written on 3 different continents of Africa, Asia, and Europe. The books were written over a period of 1500 years, in three different languages.

What's more, this collection of books shares a common storyline- the creation, fall, and redemption of God's people; a common theme – God's universal love for all of humanity; and a common message – salvation is available to all who repent of their sins and commit to following God with all of their heart, soul, mind and strength.

As you study His Word allow the Holy Spirit to speak to you. The silent but gentile tug at your heart is God. He loves you for we are His children, His creation. His first fruits.

CHAPTER 6

❧ ❧

YOUR ANSWER IS IN HIS WORD

The inspired Word of God can solve all problems in your life. It is our guide book; it is our road map; it is our compass; it is our altimeter; it is our GPS; it is our directory before things go wrong and problem solver after they do. If we will but use His Word, the Bible, our life can become simple and happiness will follow. I urge you to give it a try.

Let each of life's problems be eliminated or resolved by the Word of God. Accept this challenge, read the Word and ask God to hear your voice. His Word will speak to you if you will open your heart with praise and thanks. All of your problems can be fixed without an attorney. Let God do your battle in His Holy court for He is the final judge.

When we commit our minds to holy thoughts, we are submitting our minds to the Holy Spirit's control. This opens the way for a life of service to God and closes the door to the untold suffering that comes when we are disobedient.

1st John 1: (NKJV) 9; If we confess our sins, He is faithful and just to cleanse us from all unrighteousness. Verse 7; but if we walk in the light as He is in the light, we have fellowship with one another, and the blood of Jesus Christ His Son cleanses us from all sin. "God is Light" and to walk in the light will free us from the bondage of sin. The blood of Jesus Christ is the antidote for our defense against sin's presence and power. John also assures us that when Jesus sets us free, we are free indeed!

I perceive eventually, all Christians will come to realize that God is not foolish! He has filled the Bible with many generous promises of all the things He will do for His children. But He was wise enough to build perfect controls into His Word. We can obtain only limited answers to our prayers until we learn to keep His Word! Many Christians put a lifetime of effort into trying to "release faith" to get God's directions. It doesn't matter how enthusiastically someone tells us that we can receive everything from God simply by claiming His promises. It simply isn't true that you may have already discovered. Every promise of God is conditioned on our obedience and faith. Jesus clearly said that He received everything

He prayed for because He always did God's will.

There are several scriptures that deal with this:
1. If you abide in me, and my words abide in you, you will ask what you desire, and it shall be done for you. Found in John 15: 7.
2. And whatsoever we ask, we receive from Him, because we keep His commandments and do those things that are pleasing in His sight. 1st John 3: 22.
3. You ask and do not receive, because you ask amiss, that you may spend it on your pleasures. Adulterers and adulteresses! Do you not know that friendship with the world is enmity with God? Whoever therefore wants to be a friend of the world makes himself an enemy of God. James 4: 3-4.
4. Being in Christ's will is clearly a requirement for receiving from God. Pure desires are pleasing in God's sight! Jesus made it clear that adultery in the heart was as destructive as the act of adultery.
5. Draw near to God and He will draw near to you. Cleanse your hands, you sinners; and purify your hearts, you double-minded. James 4: 8. "You Purify" means we are capable, and we cannot expect

miraculous answers to prayers until we purify our heart.

1. Consecrate yourselves therefore, and be holy, for I am the Lord your God. Leviticus 20: 7.

2. Just as He chose us in Him before the foundation of the world, that we should be holy and without blame before Him in love. Ephesians 1: 4

3. Therefore, having these promises, beloved, let us cleanse ourselves from all filthiness of the flesh and spirit, perfecting holiness in the fear of God. 2nd Corinthians: 7.

4. Pursue peace with all people, and holiness, without which no one will see the Lord. Hebrews 12: 14

If your spiritual lives are in a rut, and you are trying method after method; prayer after prayer; year after year; there is only one way that will work; seeking holiness of heart, mind, soul and imagination. God will honor every step we take toward becoming what He wants us to be. I ask you what God wants you to be. What is His plan for you? Do you know where your path will lead? Is He the lamp unto your feet and a light unto you path?

Many books have been written and many sermons preached exhorting us not to: commit adultery, steal, hurt others, drink alcohol, etc. We have also been frequently told to; go to church, help others, care for our families, study the Bible, feed the poor, etc. These are good things, but if we never do wrong and always do good, we will still be a long way from the holiness described in the Bible.

In this generation, little has been written or taught about our need to be pure in heart, thought and imagination. The Bible filled with God's exhortations to be pure in our desires and thoughts. It is in this area that we win the real victories.

To concentrate our energies on what men do, is like sending all our fire-fighting equipment outside the city to put out brush fires, when the heart of the city itself is burning down!

The hearts of Christians are being corrupted by the world in which we live. Men and women are being sucked into the filth of lustful, adulterous, covetous thinking, and the only warning Christians are receiving is not to do any of the physical acts! Of course we are not supposed to do the acts, but we shouldn't be indulging in the thoughts either.

Immoral thinking drains away the spiritual power and life we should be living. Satan knows this and he uses his most skillful tactics to keep our inner decay from being called exactly what it is; disobedience to God. God will pour out His Spirit upon us as His Spirit controls us. Our moral decay will prevent the great revival (this is for born-again Christians) we need for the return of this country to God.

The Holy Spirit is ready to minister His fullness to each one of us as we are ready. If we are willing to work God's perfect will in our lives. Only after we become obedient will God perform His will through us.

God is angry that mankind's desires are impure. This corruption is handed down from generation to another. Be sure our sins will find us out and it is true we will reap what we sow. We must accept God's guidelines to be His followers. We must renew our minds daily focusing on Christ's character. The desire to please God should be stronger than self-gratification. When man sins his desires come under the authority of evil forces. The evil one of darkness delights in our human desires but God says be strong in His Spirit and feed upon the power of the Holy Ghost. If you try to mix the wrong things (sin) with the teachings of Christ our obedience need to be questioned. It is impossible to serve two masters. False teachers will be dealt with. The Bible was written for mankind. Mankind was not made for the Bible. A-Man?

I am so grateful God did not give up on me. His grace is sufficient to deliver us from the bondage of sin. He defeated death and is the Living God to this day. In Matthew 28: (NKJV) 5-7; But the angel answered and said to the women, "Do not be afraid, for I know that you seek Jesus who was crucified. He is not here; for He is risen, as He said, come, see the place where the Lord lay. "And go quickly and tell His disciples that He is risen from the dead, and indeed He is going before you into Galilee; there you will see Him. Behold, I have told you."

Our human understanding is so limited that we can't possibly grasp the magnitude of God's plan and purpose for us. If our understanding had to come before our acceptance, we would never be able to accept or understand His plan. However God's Word makes it clear that to understand we must first accept Christ. Pray for the wisdom of understanding believing His plan of the gospel and go forth to spread the Great Commission. Acceptance comes before understanding. As you kneel before God thank Him for who you are. Give Him praise for your life no matter how bad it seems. Thank Him for the bad things as well as the good. Once you do this a Spiritual Warfare has begun and God has never lost a battle.

If your life is full of difficulties and temptations, then be happy, for when the way is rough, your patience has a chance to grow. So let it grow, and don't try to get out of your problems. For when your patience is finally

in full bloom, then you will be ready for anything; strong in character, full and complete.
James 1: (NKJV) VERSES 2-4 says it this way;
My brethren, count it all joy when you fall
into various trials, knowing that the testing of
your faith produces patience. But let patience
have its perfect work, that you may be perfect
and complete, lacking nothing.

God has a very special plan for your life. It
began long ago when He first created you. He
formed you lovingly, carefully, exactly to His
specifications, every detail just as He wanted.
Your looks, your abilities, your place of birth,
the family you were to be born into; nothing
about you or your life has been accidental. In
love He reached out and drew you to Himself
through circumstances He had arranged just
for that purpose.

You were given a new birth, new life through
His Holy Spirit when you accepted His Son,
Jesus Christ, as your Savior, and were baptized, saturated with the Holy Spirit. And now
God's plan is to make you full and complete.
Romans 5: (NKJV) 2; through whom also we
have access by faith into this grace in which
we stand, and rejoice in hope of the glory of
God. Romans 12: (NKJV) 1-2; I beseech you
therefore, brethren, by the mercies of God,
that you present your bodies a living sacrifice. "Holy, acceptable to God, Which is your
reasonable service; And do not be conformed
to this world, but be transformed by the

renewing of your mind, that you may prove what is that good and acceptable and perfect will of God.

It is no accident that we are present with one another. God will use a willing vessel and especially one that is obedient. Obedience is better than sacrifice. Life is too short not to accept the Son of Man, the Son of God, as your personal savior. His offer is free to those that will only believe upon His name and accept His resurrection. His defeat of death on the cross paves the way, the truth and the path. Accept Jesus as your personal Savior if you haven't already done so and receive eternal life. Your answer is in His Word.

LET US MATURE IN CHRIST

Spiritual immaturity is a result of not studying the Bible or growing from faith to faith. Are you the Christian that says, "Yes", I go to church every Sunday and bless my food but do not study His Word or seek His face in prayer and supplication. Does your faith go out the door on Monday, until you can refuel next Sunday? You most likely are still a bottle fed Christian and have not accepted your discipleship with Christ. Are you a carnal Christian? Do you put on your Sunday face to get the fuzzy feeling brought about by the brief praise and worship on Sunday, and return to the Secular World on Monday? If so you need to repent of your un-belief for God demands more of His children.

Hebrew 5: (NKJV) 12; talks about "spiritual immaturity";

For though by this time you ought to be teachers, you need someone to teach you again the first principles of the oracles of God; and you have come to need milk and not solid food.

Verse 13; For everyone who partakes only of milk is unskilled in the word of righteousness, for he is a babe.

Verse 14; But solid food belongs to those who are of full age, that is, those who by reason of use have their senses exercised to discern both good and evil.

Satan loves the weakness of the "carnal" Christian. His influence in their life comes when this type of Christian fails to know what God says about protection. He fails to take discipleship to the level God intended and His son taught while here on earth. Foundational principles of the spiritual life are not to be laid again but built upon; May I repeat, "NOT TO BE LAID AGAIN BUT BUILT UPON". Why lay a foundation of a house, tear it down and do it again?

Only those who have recently accepted Christ need to be nourished by milk. It is in this tinder time we are learning to crawl, walk and then run with confidence in our Lord. This is a time when mature Christians need to offer a willing hand and become teachers. The commitment to Christ is surrounded by pitfalls and is being watched by Satan, himself.

This continuous apprenticeship as a disciple of Christ can only be finished by our faith of the cross and not after the flesh. If you ever completed an apprenticeship you know your pay will increase as you "top out" or finish the "race". It is the same when you become a follower of Christ, not a "CARNAL CHRISTIAN". People attend college for the security and money reward offered by the training. Why would they not accept the training of the Word, for its rewards are for eternity? Our Lord is sufficient in all things of this world as well as the life of eternity.

The peril of not progressing your foundations of a spiritual life is cover in Hebrews 6: (NKJV) 1 and 2; Therefore, leaving the discussion of the elementary principles of Christ, let us go on to perfection, not laying again the foundation of repentance from dead works and of faith toward God.

Verse 2; of the (doctrine) of baptisms, of laying on of hands, of resurrection of the dead, and of eternal judgment.

Yes the dead can still be raised by God.....

Mankind's addictions are nothing more than flaw or weakness brought on by immaturity. It is our want and need to take part of or participate in the practice of a false satisfaction or excitement that is not real. It has been used by Satan for centuries to gain control and enable the bondage or yoke to keep us suppressed. To be under his control will remove happiness, accomplishment, and peace from your life. The simple act of a bad habit can lead to a soft core addiction and then your mind will be taken to hard core dependency.

We must walk in the spirit: Romans 8: (NKJV) 1-6 TELLS US WHY; There is therefore now no condemnation to those who are in Christ Jesus, who do not walk according to the flesh, but according to the Spirit.

Verse 2; for the law of the Spirit of life in Christ Jesus has made me free from the law of sin and death.

Verse 3; for what the law could not do in that it was weak through the flesh, God did by sending His own Son in the likeness of sinful flesh, on account of sin: He condemned sin in the flesh,

Verse 4; that the righteous requirement of the law might be fulfilled in us who do not walk according to the flesh but according to the Spirit.

Verse 5: For those who live according to the flesh set their minds on the things of the flesh, but those who live according to the Spirit, the things of the Spirit.

Verse 6; For to be carnally minded is death, but to be spiritually minded is life and peace.

In summary if you are "carnally minded" you are enmity against God and cannot please God in the flesh.

HOW TO WALK IN THE SPIRIT

Do you need to engage the Spirit or usher in its presence?

Do you know how to use Gods presence or His word to healing?

These are questions we all have asked and especially when we need His presence. His presence is needed at all times in order to walk or dwell in Gods Holy atmosphere. We are told to pray without ceasing. We are told to seek the Kingdom and His Face. We must remain righteous and pure at heart. To remain in the Word is necessary. To be obedient to the unction of the Holy Ghost is of course a given. It is through practicing prayer daily and listening to His voice at all times that will bring the fullness of God to a mature Christian. It is simply having the faith of a mustard seed. If you are in the Spirit you won't have to call 911 or ask someone to pray for you because God is right there for you.

The guide lines for growth in the Holy Spirit are the key to living under God's grace. Only the indwelling Holy Spirit can fulfill the law through us as its guidance is requested.

Being in the Spirit will attract others that recognize the presence of the Holy Spirit. For the Spirit lives in each of us that are followers of Christ and the Holy Ghost excitement will prevail. But we are told in God's Holy Word when two or more are in unison followers of Christ and gathered in His name He will orchestrate or act upon the spoken Word, "rhema" of His children. Sometimes we will refer to this as Holy Ghost Bumps, chicken skin or a chilling of the skin that will cause the very hair to stand stiffly up. Yes for those unbelievers this is only one way we know of His presence. Some will simply say, "I feel it in my Spirit". To pray in the Spirit is one of the most awesome experiences I know. It is the border-line of prophecy. It doesn't have to be fancy words but it must be from the heart and soul. To go into the Holy Realm and approach the throne room into what we call now the supernatural for a word from God.

Matthew 18: (NKJV) 19-20; Again I say to you that if two of you agree on earth concerning anything that they ask, it will be done for them by My Father in heaven.

Verse 20; "For where two or three are gathered together in My name, I am there in the midst of them."

Often in prison church as we close and form a circle holding hands the Holy Spirit takes over. Some weep, others speak their Holy language to God and I can assure you everyone knows God is there. Yes we take advantage of the glory cloud and His Holy presence to continue our praise as other begin to lift up the desires of their heart.

The incarcerated know the apostle Paul wrote 25% of the New Testament from prison walls. Was that part of his destiny or ministry even thousands of years ago?

Paul, the apostle, the missionary wrote the book of Romans even before he went to Rome. We are told that he was probably in Corinth. I actually found a game stone under a cliff in Corinth when I was there. It resembles the same ones I have found here in America played with by the native Indians in America.

My great grandmother was Indian. Her name was Margret Lightfoot. She was on my Dads side and they were married in North Carolina. My friend Roscoe I worked with many years ago use to tell me, "you can't be all white" Tommy Joe. He is right.

Paul apparently had the same problem we do with "walking in the Spirit" for he comments in Romans 7: (NKJV) 14-20;

For we know that the law is spiritual, but I am carnal., sold under sin.

For what I am doing, I do not understand. For what I will to do, that I do not practice; but what I hate, that I do.

If then, I do what I will not to do, I agree with the law that it is good.

But now, it is no longer I who do it, but sin that dwells in me.

For I now that in me (that is, in my flesh) nothing good dwells; for to will is present with me, but how to perform what is good I do not find.

For the good that I will to do, I do not do; but the evil I will not to do, that I practice.

Now if I do what I will not to do, it is no longer I who do it, but sin that dwells in me.

Paul is saying here that the law is "spiritual" and that he is "carnal", under sin which is our human fleshly patterns. He desires to walk in the "spirit" but doesn't practice it constantly. He says it is no longer I who do it, but sin that dwells in me and this comes about when we repent and continue to do those things we repented of. Thus the changing of our mind (repenting) lacks the sincerity and conviction needed.

START HERE TO WALK IN THE SPIRIT

1. Repent and Die to Sin.
2. Live as Christ daily unto death.
3. Have no other gods before you.
4. Love thy neighbor as thy self.
5. Increase Faith beyond the portion each of us was given. Possess that "childlike faith".
6. Obey the unction of the Holy Spirit.
7. Be righteous, pure and walk in Love.
8. Diligently pray and study the Word of God.

LET US REST IN THE LORD

THERE REMAINS, THEN, A SABBATH-REST FOR THE PEOPLE OF GOD:

FOR ANYONE WHO ENTERS God's rest also rests from his own work; just as God did from His.

Hebrews 4: (NKJV) 9-10;

There remains therefore a rest for the people of God.

Verse 10; For he who has entered His rest has himself also ceased from his works as God did from His.

Most of us think of the Sabbath, (observed on Sunday for a lot of folks) as a day of rest God took after He created the universe, as recorded in the book of Genesis. That view is correct; it is the reason we should take the Sabbath, a day of rest and commanded to do so by God.

Yet the Sabbath has a larger sense; an invitation to rest in God's healing grace, trusting in His power and His purpose for your life. We rest in our Father's arms, knowing He goes before and behind, knowing that His plans for us are good and not evil.

My Grandmother Smith would prepare food before Sunday so that she and the family could spend time worshiping God. Now we just jump in the car after church and head out for our favorite restaurant. Did we forget the employees had to work and didn't even get to attend church or "rest in the Lord?"

God wants us to focus our efforts toward entering this Sabbath trust in God. It is this now-time of praise and worship He enjoys. He loves his children to be in fellowship with Him in the house of the Lord.

There was a man walking down a dusty, rural road on a hot and humid day. The man is loaded down with a heavy backpack and carries a duffle bag in each hand. A pick-up truck comes along, and the driver lets the man hop in the back. The driver heads on down the road, but when he looks in the rearview mirror he sees that his passenger is standing in the bed of the truck still holding both duffel bags still wearing the over packed backpack on his back.

Truth is: we stand in the truck of faith, still carrying our burdens, thinking they are independent of our ride with God. We think God can carry us, but not our burdens. But God's truck of faith is big enough to carry us and to carry all our burdens. Sit down and rest in the ride of God's mercy and grace as He brings us home in the Lord.

Rest on the Sabbath and fellowship with one another. Lift each other up and praise God together. Enter into the power of worship knowing God is present. The spiritual dynamic of praise will revolutionize our lives.

Martin Luther said, "blessed is he who submits to the will of God; he can never be unhappy." Men may deal with him as they will.....he without care; he knows that all things work together for good to them that love God, to them who are called according to His purpose.

Another great preacher, Charles Spurgeon said; Cry for grace from God to be able to see God's hand in every trial, and then for grace, to submit at once to it. Not only to submit, but to acquiesce, and to rejoice in it....I think there is generally an end to trouble when we get to that.

When we rest in the Lord we are renewed from the inside out. Our mind becomes more clear and functional. We begin to feel good about ourselves and develop a new zeal for the Lord. People will see the halo glow about your head. This aurora simply is Jesus coming through our actions. This new person is the same ole man but a new creature in Christ.

Moses said in Exodus 31: (NKJV) 13-14;

Speak also to the children of Israel, saying: "Surely My Sabbaths you shall keep, for it is a sign between Me and you throughout your generations, that you may know that I am the Lord who sanctifies you."

Verse 14; you shall keep the Sabbath, therefore, for it is holy to you. Everyone who profanes it shall be put to death; for whoever does a work on it, that person shall be cut off from among his people.

God established the Sabbath by ceasing the work of creation mentioned in Genesis 2: (NKJV) 2and 3;

And on the seventh day God ended His work which He had done, and He rested on the seventh day from all His work which He had done.

Verse 3; Then God blessed the seventh day and sanctified it, because in it He rested from all His work which God had created and made.

This rest and gathering should be fellowship with God and a time to bring praise to Him, for He is God our very creation and our hope of eternity. It is not a time to see or be seen by the clothes we ware. The automobile is a mode of transportation and not one to show the church members.

These thoughts go against the very fleshly patterns we have been warned of.

God commanded the Sabbath to be observed in Exodus 20: (8-11); (one of the ten commandments)

Remember the Sabbath day, to keep it holy.

Six days you shall labor and do all your work,

But the seventh day is the Sabbath of the Lord your God, In it you shall do no work; you, nor your son, nor your daughter, nor your male servant, nor your female servant, nor your cattle, nor your stranger who is within your gates.

For in six days the Lord made the heavens and the earth, the sea, and all that is in them, and rested the seventh day. Therefore the Lord blessed the Sabbath day and hallowed it.

Jesus practiced it and taught others about it mentioned in Luke 4: (NKJV) 16;

He came to Nazareth, where He had been brought up. And as His custom was, He went into the synagogue on the Sabbath day, and stood up to read.

We know that joy and blessing come from observing the Sabbath, Jesus emphasized that the Sabbath was made for people, not people for the Sabbath, Mark 2: (NKJV) 27;

And He said to them, the Sabbath was made for man, and not man for the Sabbath.

It has been made Hallowed by God but He made man for the Sabbath.

If the Body of Christ (the church people) in our country does not seek holiness of heart, there will be further decay, and the freedom of religion of worship we now enjoy will be taken away. This has happened in nation after nation since early times. God turned His back on disobedient Israel time after time.

Things on planet earth are not usually the way we would like them to be. We would like to eat what we want and never gain weight. Plant a garden and not grow weeds. Give young people good advice and see them follow it. Enjoy living but never getting old. Spend money and still have it. Change the world for the better without having to do anything for the change. The world needs to be changed. People need to be changed. We get our self into a position by trying to mix the wrong things. You cannot mix our commitment to Christ with our desires of the flesh and immoral thoughts. This combination will not be accepted by the Father.

Satanic forces are on the attack day and night, even unto our sleep.

GOD WILL SPEAK TO YOU IN
THE WIND

One night the wind awoke me as well as my spirit. I rolled out of my sleeping bag for God would not let me sleep through the Holy Ghost unction. At first I thought it was just being restless and then I realized it was God. It was about the fourth watch so I began to pray and thank Him for His presence. IT IS SO AWESOME when God wants to speak to you. The more I worshiped Him the greater the wind became and as I would be quite it would almost stop. So I grabbed my pen and began to write what God had to say.

This is how this book started as God would wake me on the fourth watch some five years ago. This is a Word from God as I Write the Words Down. I know it is for some one.

PLEASE READ THE SEQUENCE:

BEFORE FAITH YOU MUST BELIEVE.

BEFORE YOU BELIEVE, YOU MUST BE CHOSEN.

MANY ARE CALLED BUT FEW ARE CHOSEN.

THE WORD MUST BE SPOKEN SO THAT WE MIGHT

KNOW THE PATH OF SALVATION.

THE ONLY PATH TO YAHWEH IS THROUGH HIS SON, THE MESSIAH, YAHSHUA.

JESUS BECAME THE PERFECT SACRIFICE FOR MANKIND, FOR THE SCOPE OF TIME ON EARTH.

IT IS THROUGH THE HOLY SPIRIT THAT LIVES IN US THAT WE WILL BE DIRECTED IN THIS LIFE.

ONCE YOU BELIEVE, AND ACCEPT CHRIST YOU WILL BE SAVED.

THE HOLY SPIRIT WILL TAKE UP RESIDENCY IN YOUR BODY AND THUS BECOMES ITS TEMPLE.

ONCE YOU ARE SAVED, WE CAN CALL UPON THE HOLY SPIRIT FROM WITHIN TO ACCESS THE VERY POWER OF GOD.

ALL OF THE PROMISES MENTIONED IN GODS HOLY WORD IS OURS IF WE WILL BUT BELIEVE.

THE MORE YOU LEARN TO BELIEVE THE STRONGER YOUR FAITH WILL BECOME. ALL THINGS ARE POSSIBLE TO THOSE THAT BELIEVE.

GOD IS SPIRIT AND WE MUST WORSHIP AND SERVE HIM IN SPIRIT, BUT IT IS THROUGH HIS HOLY SPIRIT, HE WILL COMMUNICATE WITH US.

GOD HEARS OUR PRAYERS. WE ARE HIS CHILDREN. WE ARE HIS CHOSEN ONES. HE CALLED US. HE WILL HEAR OUR CRIES.

ACCEPT CHRIST AND RECEIVE SALVATION FOR ETERNITY.

AS THE WIND WILL ANNOUNCE HIS HOLY PRESENCE' CLOSE YOUR EYES AND OPEN YOUR EARS TO LISTEN.

WHEN YOU PRAY, YOU MUST LEARN TO LISTEN TO HIS VOICE. IT IS THROUGH THE TWO-WAY CONVERSATION OF PRAYER, GOD WILL SPEAK TO US.

USE THE HOLY SPIRIT TO TALK WITH GOD, YAHWEH.

AS YOU PRAY IT IS OKAY TO PONDER THE WORDS. TAKE YOUR TIME THAT THE RIGHT THOUGHTS GO FORTH.

WHEN THE WORDS ARE NOT PRESENT, BE STILL AND KNOW THAT GOD CAN READ THE DESIRES OF YOUR HEART.

USE THE LANGUAGE OF GOD, THE HEAVENLY UTTERANCE AND KNOW THAT GOD HEARS AND UNDERSTANDS YOUR HEART.

MANAFEST THE DESIRES OF YOUR HEART AND COMMUNICATE THEM, THROUGH THE HOLY SPIRIT.

GOD IS A LONELY GOD AND WE WERE MADE FOR HIS PLEASURE. HE WILL PUT YOU IN THE POSITION OR SITUATION YOU ARE IN JUST FOR HIS FELLOWSHIP.

PART OF BEING A CHRISTIAN IS THE PURGING OF LIFE THAT GOD WILL LET HAPPEN OR ALLOW IN ORDER FOR US TO BE MADE PURE AND ACCEPTABLE FOR THE KINGDOM.

ONCE WE RECEIVE SALVATION, WE THROUGH THE POWER OF THE HOLY SPIRIT CAN BEGIN OUR WALK WITH GOD.

IT IS THIS NOW TIME WE ARE GIVEN DIRECTION. YOUR KINGDOM COME IT WILL BE DONE ON EARTH AS IT IS IN HEAVEN.

**Your Kingdom Come Your Will
Be Done On Earth
As It Is In Heaven**

CPSIA information can be obtained at www.ICGtesting.com
Printed in the USA
LVOW111913060212

267332LV00001B/2/P